More Praise for Kelly Baader and
"A Little Girl Called Grace"

Kelly's compelling story stirred within me a familiar yet distant nostalgia of a not so distant past. The haunting narration of this book awoke deep memories of a forgotten era when girls were disadvantaged, discriminated against and considered a misfortune, having to pay the price for being born a female from cradle to grave.

Reading this book made me realize how fortunate and amazing it is that we could have come out of it sane and intact. Even more amazing is how today we can be happy, accomplished and whole, holding no animosity or bitterness, expecting no apology or recompense, just graciously able to accept that it was the way the times were back then. Kelly's story also made me realize how quickly times have changed, and how archaic those norms seem in today's context.

Her book is an inspiration for every woman facing discrimination, shame or social injustice and for every man or woman who is trapped in despair and hopelessness. Kelly navigates the reader through her story like water seeking a way through the hard mountains and dark places until he or she finally breaks through into freedom like a waterfall that gushes forth out of the side of a mountain into the sunlight.

I came to admire and respect Kelly when I worked with her while in the corporate rat race. She never fails to amaze me with her tenacity and capacity to overcome life's challenges, while at the same time remaining tender-hearted and teachable. This wonderful balance continues to help her succeed in such challenging times as she serves as a shining example of what it takes to overcome and blossom like a lotus—dignified, beautiful and whole.

—**Sara Tay,** *Woman, Wife, Mother, Investor, Friend, Director and CEO of One Heart Enterprise*

There are just some people that enter your life and feel like longtime friends the first time you meet. Kelly felt like that to me. Her warm heart and strong faith triggered an instant connection and brought us together as one in Christ. Her passion for sharing her story and desire to empower other women resonated, not just with me, but with everyone she shares it with.

It has been motivating and exciting to watch her take hold of the divinely inspired conviction to transparently share her life's journey, no matter how painful and scary it seemed. To see how God has opened doors for her and blessed her in the process is amazing! I believe her personal story is going to touch the lives of millions, especially those women who are struggling to hold on to hope when the future seems bleak, in a world where they feel unwanted and unloved. Her faith story shows just how much God loves each one of us and proves He has a unique purpose for each of our lives. It also reveals the truth of how women are still treated in many countries around the world. This is a real wake-up call for all of us.

Thank you Kelly, for stepping into the uncomfortable and painful places of your past to open up the door of grace and redemption for many. God bless you richly!

In His Grace,

—Leta Russell, *Founder of Leta Russell International, branded as the Business Launch Expert*

In a world of economic uncertainty and "doom and gloom" dominated news reports, comes a ray of hope for those who think they can't escape their seemingly hopeless situation.

"A Little Girl Called Grace" is sure to be the saving grace for many as they embark on this amazing journey with a little girl named Grace. Grace teaches us that no matter how bad the odds seem to be stacked against us, faith, hope and love can do miraculous things. This story is a must-read that will inspire and empower readers to overcome their own obstacles and move forward with a purpose-driven life.

Author Kelly Baader has already touched the lives of countless entrepreneurs as a mentor and coach and this latest project will undoubtedly give rise to a whole new crop of entrepreneurs eager to share their story and message with the world.

—Natasha Nassar, *Attorney, Author & Internet Marketing Consultant*

Just as Grace and her brother watched the other children in wonderment at the toy store, Kelly has taken all the knowledge she has gained from watching and listening to others to achieve tremendous business and personal success.

She understands that many of us have had and are still facing challenges to work through and overcome just as she has throughout her life. It is through this understanding that she tells this story; to empathize with, and then to encourage and empower others to gain the success they so deserve.

We've watched Kelly develop online under her Kelly Baader brand, and have seen her in person at empowering seminars. In person as well as in her book, she pours her heart and soul out to those who are facing struggles, and is an inspiration to the fact that no matter what our challenges… success is possible.

—**Pat & Lorna Shanks,** *Founders of TheCoolestCouple.com*

"A Little Girl Called Grace" is a powerful story about how one little girl overcame insurmountable odds and never let society or others close to her dictate her destiny. Your heart will cry out with the pain you know she experienced. Your fist will rise in anger at those you know she had to fight against. Then as you rejoice in her victory and read how she overcame each obstacle, your own mind will ask, "How can I change my destiny? Who am I allowing to dictate my worth or the person I am to become?" I know because that is exactly what happened to me.

Embrace the courage shown in this book and make it your own. Allow Grace to be your guide to let your inner light shine bright.

—**Sandy Conard,** *Founder of MultiDimension Corporation*

Kelly Baader's book, "A Little Girl Called Grace" allows the reader to relate to the trials and tribulations in their own lives. We can identify with the champion spirit that lies inside each of us through the determination of this little girl. There can be times in life when our spirit is hit so hard by life's challenges that we stop dreaming and trusting. If you've been in this place of losing your ability to see your way out of your circumstances, you will be able to glean inspiration from this little girl. "A Little Girl Called Grace," is relatable because she is you, or a loved one, family member, friend, or co-worker who gets knocked down but has the strength and faith to get back up.

This is a story about the will and determination of a little girl that keeps going, keeps moving forward, and keeps dreaming of a better life until it happens. If you are looking for the hope that you can do the same and not simply survive life but thrive in it, you are in the right place! It strengthens our belief that if she can do it, then so can we! This beautiful, strong little girl shows that with the right mindset, we not only can see our struggles as a blessing, but then use them as a way to bless others.

I give my highest recommendation to Kelly Baader. Kelly is an incredible Business Coach and friend. Her insight into what motivates people, how to bring out the best in her clients, and her ability to inspire people to take forward action has been a life changing experience for me. She epitomizes the "go-giver" mentality in everything she does, and her authentic nature resonates like a bright light. I consider myself blessed that she is my friend and coach! Thank you Kelly Baader, for reaching into our hearts and inspiring us to be our best with your book, "A Little Girl Called Grace."

—**Kimberly Schulte,** *Founder of OmmmYoga.com*

Once in a great while a book so poignant and moving comes along that it moves you to believe that there is a purpose for each of our lives—for each of our gifts! Kelly Baader's book, "A Little Girl Called Grace," will gently usher you to search inside your spirit for answers to those lifelong questions you have been seeking answers to. Kelly's story is one of courage, commitment and determination which, to this day, continues to empower her to make a difference. As "The Relational Marketer," I am constantly on the look-out for resources that continue to inspire, influence and impact. Kelly's book encapsulates these eloquently! Thank you Kelly, for your authenticity, your transparency and generosity in sharing your powerful story. I know that I know that many lives will be better because of this.

—**Emma Tiebens,** *Speaker, Author, Online Brand Strategist, The Relational Marketer*

I observed Kelly Baader from afar when I first started online and after a few months, reached out to her in friendship. We quickly realized that we had a lot of similar values and life experiences, and formed a bond of trust and respect with one another. I know that when I ask Kelly for her opinion, it is one I can count on and take to the bank.

Her story, "A Little Girl Called Grace," will touch you deeply as a woman. It is a beautiful poignant story of the trials and tribulations of a young girl growing up in a society where girls are seen as second-class citizens. You will cry when you read the parts where she is treated as worthless. You will cheer as she overcomes seemingly insurmountable obstacles. You will empathize with her as she has life experiences similar to your own. You will salute her as she reaches her true potential: A Truly Empowered Woman!

We all struggle with issues growing up, some more difficult than others. A common challenge for women is achieving the self-confidence and self-esteem necessary to rise to the top in a male dominated world. Kelly has faced more hardship than most and has still managed to become an extremely self-confident, knowledgeable and successful woman while retaining her femininity. She is a shining example of what every woman can become when they set their mind to it! She is a wonderful friend, mentor and teacher.

—**Holli Rovenger,** *Author of The Sassy Workbook Series*

Kelly is a brave and courageous woman, dedicated to freeing every woman from the cultural expectations that cause oppression and wrongly convey a message that they lack true value in the world. We share a common life's purpose as *freedom champions* in a world that stigmatizes women, often imprinting them with a poor self-image, a sense of powerlessness, and resigning them to a life of untapped potential. Kelly reminds these women that they are unique, that they matter and that they do have another choice, one that allows them to shine their light in the world. She candidly and openly shares her own struggles to matter and "make her mark" in a world that was not ready or waiting for a woman of such strength, character, tenacity and boldness. Kelly is an accomplished author and inspiring entrepreneur. I am proud to call her my friend.

—**Shan Larter**, *Founder Eating Disorder FREEDOM Coach, Eating Disorder FREEDOM Movement*

Kelly's book is a new wave of inspiration. It will give women a renewed sense of hope, especially those who are on a quest to regain their own identity and voice, and then lead other women to do the same. It is a new movement that women can be a part of. It is a spiritual guide to help wake us up and understand Who is really in control of our individual lives. Personally, it gave me goose bumps and brought tears to my eyes as it really touched my heart. I see this book being made into a movie. It is a change women want to see in life. It is about the "ultimate love" we can all receive from above; mercy, love, and joy.

—**Tatyana Gann,** *Publicist, Founder Of SmokinHotPR PR Consulting*

A Little Girl Called *Grace*

*"**Based on a true story** of how Grace not only survived a broken childhood, rough teenage years, hurtful divorce, and living in foreign lands, but then used her past wounds as her strengths to overcome and succeed in business, marriage, and family life!"*

Kelly Baader

PRESS

an imprint of **Xulon Press**
2301 Lucien Way #415
Maitland, FL 32751
www.xulonpress.com
866.381.2665

Meet Kelly online and receive free training and bonus at

www.ALittleGirlCalledGrace.com
www.KellyBaader.com

Dedication and Acknowledgements

To my God,

Who loved me first, Who made up His mind what

He wanted to do with me before I knew Him.

Who cared for me when the earthly civilization didn't.

Acknowledgments

To my mom, Li-Chu

who was brave enough to raise me up to the best of her ability,

and willing to go through fire, be broken,

and then rise up to her true identity.

To my dearest husband, Oliver,

who has stood alongside me through all my challenges,

you are my anchor!

I love you!

To my dearest children, Sarah and Philip,

your prayers, obedience, support, help in

the household, and visions have given me the strength to

keep me on the path—I love you!

To my dearest in-law family, Kurt, Trudy, Karin, Thomas, Nicholas, Isabelle, and Jeannine,
I am forever grateful for your love, care, and
support through the years.
You all helped me to see it's possible to
have love in the family—I love you all!

To my dearest friend/sister/mentor, Sara,
what can I say about the role model you have been over
the fourteen years of tears and joy we have
walked through together?
Thank you, for being radically obedient to
God so I know I am not the only crazy one.

To all my prayer warriors through the years,
you know who you are—you picked me up when I was down,
and you sowed hope into me when I couldn't see the light.
Without you, I would not be who I am today. Thank you!

A special thank you to Blake Conover,
for transcribing the first draft of this book
from my audio recording.
God says to tell you to continue to exhibit
His grace to the younger generation
and shine brightly for Him!

Special thanks to Mike Klingler, Barbara Silva, and the Coaching Cognition family.

Thank you for your encouragement and support
when I felt I couldn't move forward one more step.
It sustained me and allowed my light to shine!

Special thanks to Richard & Bridgette Bravo

Thank you for your obedience to the Lord, your creativities
and expertise which enables us to present this
project with excellence! I love you guys!

Table of Contents

Prologue

P eople who know me know I am not about converting a person's belief. I strive to share what I know through what I have experienced, and trust it will bring the seed of hope to those who hear and read it. What you are about to read might seem foreign and a bit crazy to you, but that's okay. My desire is to simply share this story with you from an authentic place of my heart. It's not about hype and weird spiritual stuff. I am just an ordinary person like you. As you will read in this story, you will see I have made a lot of mistakes and have failed many times. As we all go through the inevitable trials and tribulations of life (no one is exempt), what I have found is each one of us is broadcasting a message/story to the world around us whether consciously or unconsciously. Your story might be different than mine, but if we boil it all down and strip everything off, all we are really trying very hard to do is protect our loved ones and keep ourselves out of "trouble." Human nature is to "survive."

However, since life is not perfect, sometimes it really hurts! What's left inside of us after the "trouble" has happened is based on whether we choose to "give in" saying, "That's life, life goes on anyway," or we determine to use the pain, suffering, hardship as the amplifier to spread the seeds of hope to others. When life hurts the most, that's when our message can be delivered at its loudest level! For me personally, that is what God's grace has done for me. Now ask yourself, ***"What kind of story am I broadcasting?"***

A side note: *I purposely changed the names of people, locations, and few timelines to protect the privacy of others.* Most of the content from this book is based on my own personal story. The bottom line is, it did happen and God did show up!

Preface

My Seven-year Project

I t was about 5:00 a.m. on November 9, 2004; it was my birthday. I was sitting in our dining room with my morning coffee in my hands and thanking God for another year of my life. I opened up my journal ready to let God speak to me when I sensed someone tap on my shoulder. I turned around expecting it to be my husband up early to wish me Happy Birthday, but there was no one there. I turned back to my journal and that "someone" came and tapped on my shoulder again. This time I couldn't move!

"Kelly, happy birthday!"

"Thank You, Lord," I managed to say as I realized I was being "visited" by God Himself.

"What do you want for your birthday from Me?" He gently asked.

I surely wasn't prepared to answer such a profound question. In my mind there were thousands of things and burdens I'd like to let out. We, as a family, had just written a letter to God a few nights ago as a faith declaration for some seemingly unbelievable desires in our lives.

Somehow I was able to refrain from reiterating that list and said instead, "Father, if you could give King Solomon all that wisdom, and You say in the Bible that You are no respecter of persons, I'd like to ask for the wisdom, too. But not only for me, please also grant it to my husband and my children."

I was shocked by my own words, however I felt there was a big grin on His face.

"Kelly, what you asked is granted to you! And by the way, those things you guys asked for in your letter are granted as well."

I was speechless, totally overwhelmed by His love!

"Kelly, can you do something for Me?" He asked.

"Of course, Father," I answered, glad I could do something for the God of the universe.

"It's time to plan out the book," He told me.

"What book, Lord?" searching my mind.

"A Little Girl Called Grace," He said as I wrote the name in my journal. "It's your story, daughter!"

"Lord, I don't think it will be interesting for people to read," I answered.

"You will see," He said patiently, "Just keep it in mind as I show you something."

I was brought to a vision where I was walking up a gigantic staircase to meet God. When I finally got to the top, He gave me a hug before we sat down somewhere very high up, and swung our legs over the side while we were chatting. From out of nowhere, He took out a stack of books and asked me to throw the books down one-by-one. I wondered why He wanted me to throw the books down. As I looked down, I saw a countless multitude of people, stretching out their arms and waiting for me to throw down the books. As quickly as it had begun, the vision ended and I was back in my dining room once again.

Since then, I have carefully recorded the events of our lives as God has brought me back to those very painful memories of my past. Just when I thought I was healed from them, He would allow me to go through my most inner being to see what was really going on at that time in my life. Oftentimes the process was full of brokenness and scars, but that's when I found true wholeness.

As I finish writing this book, it is November of 2011. I realize it has been seven years since God told me to write this book! Seven is the number of completion. I trust it's part of the reason why I needed to finish writing this book by the end of my birthday month! God always has His mysterious way of accomplishing His plan.

By the way, I have enclosed a few questions at the end of each chapter designed to make you personally ponder, or to use as a guide if you are doing a group study to encourage group members to openly share from their hearts. There are no right or wrong answers. They are just to give an opportunity to each reader to dig deeper into his or her inner self, and allow the true healing to begin.

What God did for me He will do for you. So be whole!

If you are ready, let's time-travel back to Taiwan, Asia in the 1960s....

This was a time in history where men were considered far superior to women and society catered to the men. Women were thought to have little significance; their only purpose was to produce offspring. Whenever a baby was born in Taiwan, the family would have a celebration. If the child was a boy, friends and family would lavish the child with gifts. The only gifts a girl child received were eggs; symbolizing her sole purpose was to grow up, marry and reproduce. One little girl faced the difficult challenges of growing up in such a culture and rose above what society told her she could be. She never let circumstances get in her way and now she stands as an example to provide hope for women everywhere. This is the story of ***A Little Girl Called Grace.***

Chapter 1

Learning What Women Are Worth

G rowing up in a home where her mother and father were not married, Grace experienced continual dysfunctional family issues. Her mother, Anne was twenty years younger than her father who had several mistresses; of which her mother was one. When Grace was about three years old, she lived in a small apartment with her mother, father, grandmother, and another one of her father's mistresses whom she was told to call, Aunty Su. Grace could not understand why her father often spent more time with Aunty Su than he did with Anne. Su would sleep very late every day, and it was Grace's job to go and wake her at lunch time. Grace thought it peculiar for someone to sleep so late, but everyday around noon, Grace would go to Su's room and say, "Lunchtime, Aunty Su." One day, however, when Grace went to wake Su she did not get up.

"Come on, Su. Get up," said Grace's father, who had come up behind her.

Innocently, Grace mimicked her father saying, "Come on, Su. Get up."

Her father slapped her hard across the face shouting, "How dare you not call her Aunty Su! You are a disrespectful child."

As Grace fell back against the wall, tears began to roll down her face. She didn't think she had done anything wrong. If her father could say it, why couldn't she? Grace was soon to discover there a lot of things she was not permitted to do, simply because she was a girl.

Grace was a very shy young girl. If anyone would come to the house, even someone she knew, she would run away and hide. Anne tried everything to get Grace to speak to guests and neighbors, but Grace's crippling fear of other people only grew. Her antisocial behavior progressed until her mother decided that it was time for Grace to start kindergarten.

On her first day of school, Grace was terrified. As they entered the school and walked towards the classroom, her heart began to beat unnaturally faster. When her mother opened the door and they entered the room, Grace's eyes grew wide with fear. There were so many children! Grace tried to hold back the tears, but overwhelmed by fear she began to cry uncontrollably. Trying everything she could think of, Anne could not get Grace to calm down. In fact, her efforts only worsened the situation as Grace began to scream hysterically. Nervous that Grace would upset the other children, the teacher arranged for her to come back to be tested on her colors, shapes, numbers and letters once all the other children had left the room.

Grace was not nervous about the test for she had been practicing with her grandmother at home. She waited very patiently almost two hours while all the other children finished their tests and left. When it was Grace's turn, she calmly went in and sat down at a desk in the center of the room while her mother waited outside. The teacher proceeded to give her the test which did not take Grace long to finish. She knew the answers for her grandmother had quizzed her very thoroughly. When the test was complete, her teacher went out to tell Anne that Grace had passed and with very high scores. As they headed back home, Grace replayed the day in her mind. Though the morning's anxiety was not something she wished to relive, she did enjoy taking the test. She liked her teacher very much and thought perhaps school wouldn't be so bad after all.

A Brother

When Grace was four years old, her mother once again became pregnant. She and Su went into the hospital at the same time. Su was also pregnant but she was getting an abortion. While Grace's father waited for Su and Anne, he was visited by a friend of Anne's who gave him a box of very precious and expensive Korean ginseng to give to her. When her friend visited her after Anne had given birth, she mentioned to Anne that she had a box of ginseng which she had given John to give to her.

After Anne was allowed to leave recovery, she went in to see Su who had just had her abortion operation. When Anne walked in the room, she saw that the box of ginseng that was meant for her had been given to Su instead. Hurt and confused, she gave her regards to Su and then quickly left the room as tears fell from her eyes. Why was Su treated so much better than she was? Why was she given all of John's attention and affection? The more she thought about the situation, the more she asked herself, "Why do I continue to let myself be put through this by staying with him?"

Grace's father, though not necessarily a bad man, discriminated strongly against women, as did most men at that time. Consequently, he treated his family unjustly and favored his son— Grace's brother, Michael. One day, about a year after Michael was born, he and Grace were playing with blocks on the floor. Their father was sitting nearby reading his newspaper. Out of nowhere, Michael began to cry. Without seeing what had happened, John walked over and slapped Grace across the face again.

"What did you do to your brother?" he asked sternly.

"N-nothing," said Grace as she suppressed her tears.

She could never understand why her father treated her with such disrespect and contempt. It hurt her that he never seemed to care anything for her. Her father hadn't seen what happened, but he didn't have to. Grace was a girl and girls did not deserve respect—at least not to him.

Upon hearing of this incident, Anne decided it was time to move out. She didn't want herself or her family subjected to John's actions anymore. She couldn't explain to Grace what was happening, but she knew she had to secretly pack their things and leave right away. The next day, Grace was sent to school as usual, but was surprised to see her mother and Grandmother outside the window talking to one of the teachers.

Minutes later, the teacher opened the classroom door, leaned in and said, "Grace, come see who is outside."

Grace stood, a bit confused, and made her way out of the classroom. She was surprised to see that both her mother and grandmother were carrying large suitcases. They looked worried.

As Grace reached them, her mother bent down to her and whispered, "Grace, I cannot explain what is happening, but you must hurry and gather your things. We are leaving."

Though confused, Grace did not ask questions. She quickly did as she was told. After leaving the school, they rushed to the airport and caught a flight to Kaoshung in South Taiwan. During the flight, none of them spoke, but Grace saw the anxious looks on both the women's faces and it worried her. Where were they going? Why couldn't they have said good-bye to anyone? Were they coming back? "Perhaps we're taking a vacation," Grace thought to herself. With that pleasant idea in mind, she thought no more about it and enjoyed the rest of the flight.

When they arrived in Kaoshung, they went to see a friend of Anne's named Kate. She offered to let them stay with her and her husband until they could find a place of their own. Though Grace still did not fully understand, she soon realized that this was not a vacation. She quickly became accustomed to sleeping on the floor, for there were no more rooms in the house.

A New Life

During this time, Anne began looking for a job. Though no one knew what kind of job she was looking for, she would be out most of the day searching. Most days, she would leave very early and return home worn out and stressed just before dinner time. Dinners were normally quiet though Kate would often try to make conversation by asking questions. More often than not she was met with one-word answers or a simple shrug.

Though quite young, Grace was very intelligent. She began to notice that Kate's husband would stare at Anne during mealtimes and go out of his way to talk to her for extended periods of time when Kate was not around. Grace could sense that this made her mother uncomfortable.

Anne began to speak more often of leaving saying, "Soon I shall have a job and then we can find a place of our own and we won't have to bother you anymore."

Kate's husband often looked displeased with such statements, but said nothing. Soon it became quite obvious that he had affections for Anne. One night after dinner when Grace was getting ready for bed, she made her way to the kitchen to say goodnight to her mother, but Kate's husband had reached Anne before Grace could.

"You look tired." he said to Anne as she leaned against the counter with her head in her hands.

"You work yourself too hard," he said as he began rubbing her shoulders.

Grace watched as Anne quickly shrugged him off.

"Why are you in such a hurry to get a job? You only stress yourself out. Relax, take your time. You know you can stay here as long as you need," he said in a comforting voice.

"That is very kind of you," Anne replied without looking up at him, "but I will not allow us to overstay our welcome. I must find a job as soon as possible. Then we will no longer burden you and your wife. You have been so kind to us already."

"Burden?" he responded with a chuckle. "It is never a burden to have such a beautiful woman staying in my home. I hope you will consider staying longer."

When Anne didn't respond, He moved closer to her and slowly ran his hand down her arm, "I would very much like it if you did."

"Shouldn't you be with your wife?" Anne responded as she quickly pulled away from him.

"This is my house. I can be wherever I want and I can do whatever I wish," he said as he got even closer to her.

Anne angrily pushed him away saying, "Sir! You are a married man. And unless you would like me to tell your wife of your behavior, I ask that you keep your distance. We will be out of your hair soon enough."

With that, she turned to leave the kitchen for the first time seeing Grace standing there. Extremely uncomfortable with what her daughter had just witnessed, Anne sighed heavily as she went to put Grace to bed. Though Grace was obviously confused, Anne could not explain things to her young daughter but simply assured Grace that everything was alright and that soon they would be living in their own home.

After the incident in the kitchen, Anne decided it was time for them to leave, with or without a job. They had no idea where they were going to stay, but she knew they could not stay there any longer. Early the next morning, they were all packed and ready to leave. They said good-bye, thanked Kate and her husband for their hospitality, and left in search of a place to call their own. They found a small apartment where the rent was low enough that Anne could use what little money she had left to keep them until she found a job.

What About Michael?

Around this time, they began receiving a series of letters and messages, though Grace was never told who they were from or what they were about. One night, as Grace was falling asleep, she heard her mother and grandmother talking. Peeking out from under her blanket, she listened and watched as they talked about the mysterious envelopes.

"We cannot go back," said her grandmother.

"Well, we can't just leave Michael there either. Besides, do you really think John will stop trying to get in contact with us if we don't go back? Look at all these letters," Anne said as she motioned to the stack of letters on her lap. "He won't leave us alone."

"Then write him back, but I don't see why we should have to go all the way back there only to leave again," her grandmother argued, "you should respond to his letters, but that's it."

"If we respond, then he'll only be more inclined to continue writing us. And what about Michael?" protested Anne.

"What about Michael?" her grandmother argued. "John obviously loves him which is more than he does any of us. He will treat Michael well. Why do you feel so strongly that we must go back for him?"

"He is my son, too! I'll no longer allow John to influence me or my family. I want him out of our lives and out of Michael's life, too," Anne said firmly, "I don't want Michael to grow up to be just like his father. We're going back."

With that the discussion ended, but Grace now knew why they had left her father's house. All these years she had thought her mother and father loved each other. This information upset her greatly, though she would never mention it to her mother or her grandmother. She thought about the things she had heard as she slowly drifted off to sleep.

Later that week, the family packed up again and headed back to John's house. When they arrived, Su answered the door with a smile, but upon seeing them her smile turned to a frown.

"Oh, it's you," she said with a look of disapproval.

She just turned her back and walked away, leaving the door open for them to let themselves in. When John arrived home from work later that evening, he was shocked to find them there.

"I knew you would come back eventually," he said to Anne. "I'm glad you've finally realized where you belong."

"Yes, I have," Anne replied, "which is why we're not staying."

"What do you mean you're not staying?" John's face turned red with rage as he asked, "Where will you go? You have no money and no one would accept the burden of taking you in. This is your home. Here you can at least be certain that you will be sheltered and fed. This is where you belong."

"Though we have shelter and food here, we are not safe from you," Anne said with more confidence than she felt, "All you've done is make us miserable. I don't want that for Grace and I'm tired of being unhappy. I want to be free."

"You think you'll be happy and free when you're penniless, living on the streets?" John sneered.

"Free from you at least," Anne boldly replied.

"Well, if you despise me so much, why did you return?" John asked sarcastically.

"To get my son," Anne declared, "I don't want him to grow up with only you as an influence; having no respect for women and treating people however he wants. I can't stand the thought of him becoming just like you."

"No, you will not take Michael. He is my son and he belongs to me, as do all of you!" John commanded. "However, I shall allow you to leave if you must, but I'll not take you back when you're poor and homeless."

He then turned and walked away. Looking at Michael, Anne's heart ached. Michael was eating a big pack of candy given to him by Su. The thought of how they had been taking care of her son prompted Anne to come up with a backup plan and she agreed to stay. Nearly a week later, Anne put her plan into action. Anne knew John wanted Michael to stay with him and would not let him leave, so she waited until late at night when John and Su were asleep. Then she gathered Grace, Michael, and their grandmother and left with only the moonlight to guide them.

After arriving back in Kaoshung, they then began moving from apartment to apartment. They moved so often, Grace could hardly distinguish one place from the next as they all blurred together in her mind. She grew tired of the constant moving and couldn't understand why they never stayed in one place for very long. Grace was soon to learn what it was like to grow up without a father.

Ask Yourself

- If you were Grace, what perception would you have concerning the value of woman versus a man at this time in Grace's life?

- Have you ever been punished by your father or mother the way Grace was by her father? If yes, how did it make you feel?

- What kind of impact might be instilled in Grace's mind and heart if Anne had continued to live with another mistress under the same roof?

Chapter 2

Growing Up Without Father

When Grace was between seven and eight years old, they settled down in Taipei. Anne finally found a job at a hotel. However, this hotel was unlike regular hotels. Men, usually of prestige, would come in for a banquet and sit at a long banquet table with a prostitute sitting between each man. The men would eat and drink until they were satisfied, then take their prostitute and leave. This was a very foreign environment for Anne, but she worked hard and soon became the manager of sales there. She learned to drink and smoke to fit the work environment because it was customary for her to make a toast at each banquet.

Due to Anne's night shift, eight-year-old Grace would have to come home from school, help her Grandmother take care of four-year-old Michael, then do her homework. Often she was even left to care for him by herself because of both her mother and grandmother's severe gambling addiction. Though she grew to have a deep anger for her mother and grandmother's addictions and irresponsible behavior, never once did she complain. She simply did what she had to do.

Anne slowly started bringing men home. It was different man every few days. Grace didn't like having strange men around and never spoke a word to any of them. She grew more and more annoyed at her mother's behavior and couldn't understand why her mother constantly needed these men around. They would pay Anne before they left and Grace's grandmother would simply tell her that it was because her mother was just trying to provide for the family.

After months of this, Anne finally got a steady boyfriend. Her boyfriend's name was Jo and Grace was unsure of how she felt about him. He seemed nice enough, but there was something about him that made her uneasy. Soon after he and Anne started dating, Grace learned that her mother's boyfriend was already married. He and his wife were separated but they had not yet divorced. Jo had kids, though they were all grown already, the situation didn't sit well with Grace. But as she had been doing most of her young life, she kept her thoughts to herself. After all, what would a child know of adult affairs?

Things seemed to be going well with Anne and her boyfriend at first, but after a while the circumstances became very strange. Jo's business went on the decline so this put stress on him and pressure on Anne to once again be the family's sole provider in case his business totally failed. Frustration often led to fights. They would get home from work, begin to drink, and then the arguing often turned to shouting as furniture was thrown around and possessions intentionally broken. On occasions, knives would even be waved around and thrown. Grace spent many sleepless nights feeling frightened; waiting for the noise to die down. It was a difficult situation for the rest of the family. Grace would try to distract herself with school to take her mind off of the chaos at home.

School—A Place of Comfort

Grace worked very hard in school, especially in junior high. By then she had already developed a desire to prove that women weren't useless and that they were more than just "baby-production machines." Her self-motivation pushed her to excel in all of her studies. Not everything about school was easy for her though. She would often be asked by teachers why she could not provide information on her father. She was one of only a very few students whose father was not involved and this left deep emotional scars. It was a constant reminder of the fact that her father was not around and an embarrassment for her growing up.

She remembered once in second grade when her father showed up, but only because he wanted the two children to take his last name. Anne agreed to it only because he was so persistent, but once he got what he wanted he left again, and Grace didn't see him after that. It was difficult for her as she saw how happy all the kids around her were doing things with their families. She often wondered why hers was so broken. She didn't understand it and it left scars on her heart where no one could see them.

Walking down the street with Michael one Saturday afternoon, Grace came upon a toy store. It had a huge front window for passersby to look into. Michael ran over and pressed his face against the glass. Grace followed. It was amazing! Large animatronic characters waved at them from behind the glass. The store was filled with every kind of toy they could imagine. Inside Michael and Grace could see children's faces filled with glee as they selected toys off of the shelves to purchase. Grace saw one man take an action figure off the shelf and handed it to his son. The boy's face lit up as he hugged both of his smiling parents.

Upon seeing this, Grace grabbed Michael and pulled him back away from the window. Michael tugged on her arm to go back to the window but she refused watching as moments later the little boy she had been watching emerged from the store with his parents and his new toy. Grace watched longingly as the happy little family passed by them and rounded the corner out of sight. Slowly she and Michael began to make their way home. Thinking about the family she had seen made her heart sink. They looked so happy. A tear ran down her cheek as she thought of her own family. Her father was never around; she doubted he even loved her at all. Her mother even seemed to not care about her lately. None of them were ever happy. The only emotions Grace felt at home were fear and unhappiness. The only place that she ever felt a sense of peace and achievement was school.

Grace went through six years of primary school, and three years of junior high. After that, she had to compete with students nationwide to try and make it into one of the top three senior high schools in the nation. If a student did not make into one of these senior high schools, it was perceived they would likely get a low-end job. This was a very big deal to Grace. She hadn't studied hard all these years to fail now. She determinedly entered the competition knowing she was competing against over 30,000 other students to get in one of the top three high schools. It was very stressful and she became very anxious as she awaited the results from all the tests.

As Grace waited to hear the results, she grew more and more nervous as the day the results would be posted grew slowly closer. Some days she wouldn't even eat anything because she was so overcome with anxiety. After what seemed like days and days of waiting, the day she'd been anticipating was finally here. Grace could not sleep the night before and woke up very early knowing the results were to be posted at noon. Grace spent a restless morning cooking, cleaning, and doing whatever she could to keep herself occupied. She watched the clock all morning until finally noon came around.

Excited to see her results, she asked her mother, "Do you want to come with me to see if I got in?"

"No," replied Anne, trying to hide her own worry over what the results would reveal.

Grace was disappointed and a bit surprised by her mother's quick refusal. She ended up going with her close friend from school to get the results. When they arrived at the announcement board, it was surrounded by crowds of people. Parents, students and even grandparents had gathered around. The two anxious girls made their way through the crowd and squeezed to the front so they could read the board. They searched for several moments until both found their own name. They followed their names across the row to see their results. After reading their placement, the girls both screamed and hugged each other. They had both made it into the number two school!

"I can't believe it!" Grace exclaimed. "We made it!"

"How much did we miss the number one school by?" asked her friend.

Upon taking another look at the board, Grace's face dropped,

"I don't believe this!" Grace said, clearly outraged by what she read. "We missed by only 0.02 points! That's ridiculous!"

"What?" her friend exclaimed, equally indignant that they could be denied entrance for such a small grade point difference.

"I don't understand. How could such a small ratio make such a big difference?" Grace said as she looked at her friend.

After swallowing her disappointment, Grace decided to head home and tell her mother her news. As she walked back to the apartment, she began to feel better. Though she didn't make it into the best senior high school in the nation, she did make it into the second best one. Grace decided that was good enough for her. Though it was a shame to have missed the top school by such a small point margin, she was happy she made it into the number two school. This school was significant to Grace for another reason; it was the same school her mother had attended.

"Mother!" she exclaimed as she threw open the door to their apartment, "I made it! I made it into the number two school!"

Anne's face lit up as she realized that Grace would be attending the same school she had gone to herself. But for some reason after a few seconds, her expression changed back to that of less excitement.

"Tonight we shall go out to eat," Anne announced but with very little enthusiasm in her voice.

Grace noticed the rapid change in her mother's emotions and was confused thinking her mother would have been much more excited. She didn't even mention that she had gone to that very same school. But then again, it seemed her mother never really showed much excitement at anything Grace did. Perhaps, Grace thought, she really was happier than she chose to express. Despite her mother's less then enthusiastic reaction, Grace was still extremely excited and couldn't wait to start school again.

The National Day Parade

Grace soon began attending her all-girl high school where she was taught honor and how to be competitive both academically and other important areas of life. Her school participated in the huge National Day Parade with the army, navy, and air-force. The students would be trained for four months by an army trainer to do elaborate tricks with guns while marching in a precisely orchestrated cadence. Two hundred girls who had the highest grades from the top three senior high schools got to participate in the event. Upon receiving the news that she would be able to participate in the event, Grace became overwhelmed with excitement. On the first day of training, the girls were eager to get started as they raved about how much fun this was going to be!

"I hear we're being trained by a military trainer," said one of the girls.

"It's got to be pretty intense then," said another.

"How hard could it be?" Grace thought with a shrug.

The girls were quite surprised, however, that this was far more intense than any of them had expected. This event was taken very seriously and if one person dropped their gun or did the wrong motion or went in the wrong formation, it would ruin the whole performance. Everyone had to be exactly in sync with one another and they had to focus very hard on remembering their motions and formations. Mistakes would not be tolerated. Training proved to be more rigorous and repetitive than anything Grace had ever done before. She loved it though and it taught her discipline, precision, and, most importantly, teamwork.

When the big day came, Grace was very nervous. She got up very early and went to her school to meet the other girls. When their instructor arrived, they followed him to the grounds where the parade would be held and were put into formation behind the other performers in the parade. The parade was to begin at seven o'clock but people were already beginning to line the streets. By 6:30 Grace could feel her nerves starting to get to her. What if she did the wrong motion or forgot a trick? What if her timing was off? "I swear if I mess this up I'll never forgive myself!" she thought.

After what seem to Grace like hours of waiting, it was finally seven o'clock and time for the parade to start. Once the announcer had finished speaking, the music began to play. As the girls started their routine, Grace was still feeling very nervous. She was trying very hard to stay focused with all the action and noise going on all around her. As they marched by the announcer's box, Grace heard him announce them and the crowd cheered. Once Grace heard the applause, all her nerves went away and the adrenaline kicked in. She smiled widely and performed the remainder of the routine with confidence. The cheers continued as they marched down the road. Grace felt overwhelmingly honored and proud as she performed every motion and trick with perfection.

Grace was disappointed when the procession had ended and the day was over. Though she was tired, she wanted the day to continue on. It was a memorable experience for Grace to be a part of a nation-wide celebration. As she walked home, she relived the parade over and over in her mind, smiling all the way. She let out a sigh of relief, knowing she hadn't missed a beat and the celebration was a success. She had many other happy experiences as she went through her years of school but the National Day Parade was at the top of her list.

Ask Yourself

- Have you ever tried to prove to someone that they were wrong about you? If yes, what were the pros and cons of doing so?
- How important is your parents' healthy relationship with each other and with you? Can you tell what might have been going on in Grace and Michael's life as they were growing up?
- Can you relate with Grace how she loved her school instead of home? If yes, why?

Chapter 3

Entering the Wolf's Den

G race cherished her time at that school. She grew to love everyone so much. She never wanted to leave. She couldn't believe three years had already gone and there were only a few months left before graduation. It saddened her to say good-bye to all the friends she had made, all the teachers and classes she had grown so fond of. They would be memories she would cherish throughout her lifetime.

Her sadness was short-lived, however, as she was soon thrust headlong into a heated competition to get into a university. This was very important to Grace. If she didn't get into a university, she would have to settle for going to a college. Colleges weren't bad. In fact, they were very good. But universities were thought of as a higher form of education than colleges and if there was one thing Grace had learned over the years it was to never settle for less than the best you can get. She was determined to get into a university. Universities required two more years of learning than colleges, but Grace didn't care. She loved to learn and was used to earning her way competitively. This came in handy as the competition for admittance to a university was stiff.

Grace studied hard in preparation for the exam, even before graduating from senior high school. Normal school hours were 7:00 a.m. to 4:00 p.m. Most days Grace would stay several hours after school to study, then go home and study some more. She had a deep desire to learn; a seemingly unquenchable thirst for knowledge. The more information she had, the more confident she was that she would have no trouble passing her exam to get into a university.

The first day of the exam, she was very nervous. Her previous confidence was suddenly replaced by an overwhelming anxiety. "Have I studied everything? Do I have all the information I need?" she asked herself. "What if I forget all the things I've learned?" These thoughts continued to plague her all day until she came in to take her test. As she sat nervously waiting for the exam to begin she prayed quietly, "Please, God, whoever You are...let me remember everything." Her exam paper was then placed before her, and her nervousness intensified. After answering the first few questions, however, her nerves soon dissipated and she continued on with increasing confidence. When she had finished, she turned her paper in to the woman proctoring it, and exited feeling the exam hadn't been the least bit hard for her. She had psyched herself out for nothing. She continued with the same level of confidence all three days of testing. Now all that there was left to do was wait for the results.

She would be notified in three months as to whether or not she gotten in. To prepare to pay for the tuition, she decided to begin looking for a job. If she was working, she could help her mother provide for their family, as well as gain some work experience. She went out daily searching for job opportunities. She found few offers and the ones she did find had stringent requirements which Grace did not meet due to her youth and lack of experience and expertise. Finding work was proving to be a more difficult task than she initially thought.

Three months had gone by slowly as Grace eagerly awaited the acceptance letter she was fully confident she would receive from the university board. However, after several days passed and she did not receive her letter, she began to worry. Maybe she hadn't been accepted after all. But, she reminded herself, either way they would still have to notify her. As the days turned into a week with no sign of a letter of any kind, Grace became quite confused.

After nearly two weeks of waiting since she was supposed to have received the results from the university, she trudged out to check the mail with very little hope that she would find anything. Upon reaching the mailbox, she stopped, almost not wanting to open it. Slowly and timidly she reached to open it, expecting to be met with further disappointment. As she looked inside, her heart leapt. A letter was there addressed to her from the university! She swiftly grabbed it and ran back to show her family.

As she raced in the door, out of breath, she held the envelope high and exclaimed, "Look! It finally came!"

Excitedly her family gathered around as Grace seated herself on the couch and began opening the letter. Taking it out of the envelope, she read it aloud,

"Dear Miss Grace, Thank you for your patience. We appreciate your participation. We have gone over your test results very thoroughly. After reviewing your scores we are pleased to inform you that you have been accepted to our university. We look forward to seeing you."

Grace did not read the closing of the letter. She had read all she needed to. She simply sat there smiling, her face beaming. Her family all jumped up and down and lavished her with praises.

"Now my daughter can finally make something of herself!" Anne exclaimed.

To Grace's surprise, her mother was much more excited this time around than she had been when Grace got into her senior high school. But Anne had always known Grace would have no problem getting into one of the top three schools. This, however, was a much bigger deal to Anne because she knew that Grace could now become independent. She could get a high-end job and be whatever she wanted to be. Grace definitely had the motivation and work ethic to get her anywhere she wanted to go. The family spent the night in celebration of Grace's achievement and Grace was in ecstasy as she thought of university life.

I'm Your Father

The next day, everyone was in good spirits, especially Grace. As she was getting ready to leave to go job-hunting, Grace heard a knock at the apartment door. Curious, she answered it with a smile. When she saw who was standing there, she was shocked, and her cheery smile disappeared as she stared with wide eyes at the man she'd grown to despise.

"Grace who is at the door?" called Anne from the other room.

When Grace did not answer, her mother came to the door, "Grace did you…"

She stopped mid-sentence as she looked at the man in her doorway, "John, what are you doing here?"

"I came to speak with you. May I come in?" he asked.

Grace did not wish to speak with him so she said curtly, "No!" as she began to close the door.

Anne grabbed it before it closed saying, "Forgive her," as she reopened the door. "Please, come in."

Grace glared at her mother, and began to walk away.

"I came to congratulate you, Grace," said her father as he stepped into the apartment and Anne closed the door behind him.

Grace stopped before she reached the other room, turned around and walked back over to stand in front of him.

Crossing her arms in front of her, she said, "Well, now you did. Is that all you came here for?"

"Well no, not exactly. I was hoping I could persuade you all to go to dinner with me tonight," John invited.

"And why would we do that?" Grace asked, pleased that her father looked startled by her question.

Anne cut in before he could answer, "What Grace means is, though Jo and I work very hard, we barely have enough money to afford the necessities. We couldn't possibly afford going out to a restaurant."

"Of course not," John said with a hint of disdain in his voice. "I mean that I shall take you all to dinner. You won't have to pay for anything."

"Well, that's very gracious of you," said Anne, "but..."

"But we don't have time for you," Grace interrupted.

"Grace please," Anne urged, "be respectful."

"Why? When has he ever treated any of us with respect? Why should I respect a man who never cared about me—or any of us for that matter?" Grace asked with contempt in her voice.

"Grace, I do care about you," John said.

"Oh, you do!" Grace responded, as her anger threatened to boil over, "Well, that explains why I haven't seen or heard from you since I was four years old."

By this time Michael, who was now fourteen, heard the commotion and entered the room.

"What's going on?"

He froze when he saw his father, "Who are you?"

"Don't you remember me, son?" John said as he moved toward Michael, "I'm your father."

Michael looked at Grace and Anne, then back at John and asked, "If you're my father, then why haven't I met you before?"

"Your mother took you away when you were very little," said John seizing on Michael's obvious confusion.

"Why?" Michael asked as he looked at his mother.

"I did it to protect you," Anne said.

"Protect me from what?" Michael asked his mother.

"From him," Grace said as she pointed at their father.

"I still don't understand," Michael said, looking from Grace to his mother to John.

"Because he doesn't love us and he never has," Grace said with conviction.

"That's not true!" John insisted, "Michael, I do love you."

"Then why didn't you come after us?" asked Michael, realizing the truth in what Grace was saying.

"Well, I couldn't. I was—busy," John answered obviously fumbling for an excuse he thought his son would accept.

"Busy for fourteen years?" Michael asked with a wisdom beyond his years, "If you really loved us you would have found a way to at least see us once in a while."

"Children please," John pleaded, "give me a chance to prove myself."

"Prove yourself?" Grace scoffed, "I don't understand why you're suddenly trying to rekindle relationships you chose not to have. If you truly cared for us you would have shown it a long time ago. I've been waiting fourteen years for you to "prove yourself." I guess I have just gotten used to disappointment."

With that Grace turned and stormed out of the room. Michael looked at his father, shook his head, and quickly followed Grace.

Anne stood shocked in the middle of the room, "I'm sorry for their disrespect. Of course we will go to dinner with you tonight. That is very kind of you," she said as she forced a smile and opened the door for him to leave.

John nodded knowingly, "I'll see you all tonight then."

He exited the apartment and Anne quickly shut the door.

"How could you?!" exclaimed Grace as soon as her mother shut the door.

"He is your father, Grace," Anne said sternly, "You and your brother were very rude to him."

"I don't care. He's not my father. He never has been," Grace said trying to control her tears, "he never wanted to be."

"Well, he's trying to be now," Anne pointed out.

"Well, it's going to take a lot more than buying us dinner to convince me of that," Grace declared. "Don't you think it's a little late for him to try and change now? I'm eighteen, I don't need him now. I needed him when I was a child, seeing other children with both their parents and wondering why I never had that. When people would ask me about my father I could never give them an answer. Where was he when we were living in a small apartment that was barely big enough for the four of us and sleeping on the floor because we couldn't afford beds? That's when I needed him, not now."

"I know," Anne cajoled, "but you still need to honor his request by coming to dinner. He came all this way just to see you."

"Fine. I'll go," Grace said more to please her mother than anything else, "But don't think that this changes anything between him and me."

Grace and Michael reluctantly went to dinner that night, during which time John made an announcement that surprised them all, "Grace, I'd like to pay for your tuition to the university, if you don't mind."

Grace's eyes widened for a moment, then her expression went back to normal and she continued eating.

"If you wish," was all she said.

"Aren't you happy about it?" her father inquired. "It is quite a large amount of money you know."

"Why are you doing this?" Grace asked with annoyance in her voice.

"Well, because I know it will be difficult for you to come up with the money on your own and this is a token to show you that I'm proud of you," John explained.

"You're not proud of me," Grace said knowingly, "You're proud because someone with your last name achieved success and you want everyone to know that I belong to you. You're not doing this because you "care about me." You're doing it because you think you own me. Well, you don't!"

Grace swiftly stood, "You want to put your name on it so whatever success I achieve will reflect well on you. You are the only person you care about. You expect me to be happy about that? Well, go ahead and pay the tuition if you wish, but I'll have you know I never wanted your money. I wanted a father."

She marched out of the restaurant and her family quickly followed, leaving John sitting there alone and embarrassed. Grace did not speak to her father again after that, but John reassured Anne he would pay the full tuition before school started.

However, when Grace went to register for her classes at the university, the woman at the front desk asked, "And what is your payment plan?"

"What do you mean?" asked Grace, surprised by her question.

"How are you going to pay the tuition?" the receptionist explained.

"My father should have made the payment already," Grace told her, suddenly feeling sick to her stomach.

"We have no record that any payment was made toward your tuition," the receptionist assured her, "Perhaps you should speak with your father."

"I knew it!" thought Grace, "I knew he wouldn't go through with it."

She looked back at the woman at the desk and said, "No, that's alright. I'll pay it myself."

"Very well," the woman replied as she gave Grace the total she needed to register and how to set up an acceptable payment plan for the rest of her tuition.

Grace knew she had to find a job soon in order to pay for her schooling. Her lack of success in finding one so far pressured her to search harder and longer.

A Working Woman

One Saturday morning, after a long week of job-hunting, Grace got a call from one of the businesses she had applied to saying that they would like her to come back for an interview. Delighted, Grace was there early the following Monday morning.

She waited only a few minutes before the manager, Ron entered the room, "Good morning."

Grace politely returned his greeting.

"Well, I'm just going to get right to the point. We've looked over your application and we think you'd be perfect for the job."

Grace looked confused, "Just like that?"

He nodded.

"But I have no experience…," Grace said still stunned by his words.

"That's perfect," Ron replied his eyes making contact with Grace's. "We need someone who is willing to learn and work hard. Given your extensive education I take it your work ethic is excellent."

"So I got the job?" Grace asked incredulously.

"Yes," Ron affirmed, "And you can start right away."

Grace eagerly agreed and began her training that very day. Although she didn't feel quite comfortable with Ron, she looked forward to starting her new job, selling educational cassettes. Grace worked very hard and enjoyed her job. It kept her busy and she was out of the house most of the day due to school and work. She didn't like being at home as the situation with Anne and her boyfriend had been getting progressively worse. It was very stressful, and at times dangerous for the rest of the family to be around them.

Grace poured herself into learning all the techniques of good salesmanship. She became comfortable working in a big corporation and even attended some expos periodically which she started to look forward to. Grace loved all of her fellow employees and worked well with them. She also learned that Ron was just divorced and didn't have a good reputation with the ladies. "Maybe that's why I don't feel right about him," Grace pondered, determined to steer clear of him.

One man she was particularly fond of was a very kind man named Daniel who was about eight years older than her. Daniel would always go out of his way to help Grace. They talked often and Grace felt herself becoming more and more attracted to him as the days went by.

The whole sales team often travelled together to attend trade shows. This time they all checked into the same hotel and then met to prepare their presentations for the following day. During the break, Ron came to tell Grace he would like to take her out to show her around the city, and teach her some more sales techniques.

"I want to make sure my superstar does a good job presenting tomorrow," he said with a weird smile that chilled Grace to the bone.

"Can't we just do that here with everyone else?" Grace timidly suggested.

"Well, if you'd like to keep this job and receive a promotion in the near future, my personal mentorship will get you there faster for sure," Ron said, pressuring her to accept his invitation.

"Sure, boss," Grace reluctantly agreed feeling helpless to refuse!

As Ron walked smugly away, Daniel passed by and asked, "So are you ready for the big day tomorrow?"

"Well, I thought so," Grace forced out between clenched teeth, "but obviously Ron has a different opinion!"

"What do you mean?" Daniel asked seeing Grace's discomfort over the situation.

"He said he'd like to teach me some more selling techniques and take me out later to see the city," Grace explained, still feeling pressured into doing something she really did not want to do.

"Do you feel comfortable about it?" Daniel asked, looking more than a little disturbed.

"No, but it appears he is not giving me much of a choice," Grace told him. "Ron mentioned something about keeping my job and receiving a promotion. I am concerned about the consequences if I don't comply with his request."

Grace looked at Daniel, sending out a non-verbal "help me" signal.

"I'll see what I can do," Daniel said obviously aware of Ron's reputation with the ladies.

"Are you ready to go?" Ron asked later, with an authoritative tone in his voice.

Before Grace could open her mouth, Daniel stepped in and asked, "Boss, where are you going with Grace?"

"Since this is her first time for this kind of expo, I'd like to make sure she is familiar with the local market, so I am taking her out to some places and have some one-on-one training with her," Ron reluctantly replied, obviously annoyed at Daniel's interference.

Diplomatically Daniel asked, "Do you know which area you guys will be in so I can bring the rest of the team and join you later for the traditional team dinner?"

"Well, I am not sure yet. I'll give you a call when I know where we are going to end up," Ron offered, obviously not really excited about the prospect.

"But why don't you guys just go ahead, pick a place for the dinner and really enjoy yourselves without your boss around. Wouldn't that make it a lot more relaxing for the team?" Ron said jokingly, apparently intent on not joining up with the rest of the team.

Grace was so nervous, she didn't know what to say to keep from going out alone with Ron. She needed this job to pay her tuition though she smelled danger in Ron's attempts to get her away from the others. In her mind, she was silently screaming out for help from Daniel.

Daniel squeezed out a smile as he countered with, "No kidding boss, without your presence, the dinner and karaoke wouldn't be any fun. Besides, everyone wants to challenge Grace to sing some songs. We can't let Grace take the easy way out at her very first team trade show, right, Grace?"

She sent a silent thank you to Daniel as she flowed into his escape plan, "Of course not, I've been waiting for a long time to be part of this 'team karaoke' I have heard so much about. I surely don't want to miss it."

"Fair enough," Ron interrupted, "Let's get going so we can come back early enough to catch the Karaoke competition."

Pushing Grace towards the lobby entrance, Ron demanded, "Let's go, Grace!"

As Grace moved slowly forward, she looked back at Daniel who gave her an assuring look. Though puzzled she acted like she understood, seriously hoping Daniel had a plan to keep her from any alone time with Ron. They visited a few business acquaintances of Ron's and Grace kept hoping there would be a call from Daniel giving some reason for them to return to the group.

As they hopped in a taxi and Ron mentioned to her he'd like to show her something special, Grace was hoping they were finally on their way to join the others for dinner and karaoke.

"Where are we going, boss?" Grace asked.

Ron placed his hand on Grace's left knee and said, "To somewhere we can spend some quality time together."

"Boss, I don't know what you mean!" as she tried to glide away from him. "If it is not for business, then I think we should go back to the hotel and join the team."

"Come on Grace, you know I like you a lot, and this will be good for your career. I will take good care of you. Let's find some private place and enjoy ourselves, what do you think?" he said as he placed his right arm around her shoulder, and his lips upon her face.

There were thousands of thoughts flashing around in her mind as she saw the faces of Anne and Jo, how they got drunk and fought against each other. Then she remembered that happy family she and Michael had seen that day looking in the toy store window. She remembered her own abusive father's voice and how he slapped her across the face with such force it knocked her to the ground crying.

"Am I stepping into this man's control just like my mother did? Do I really want that kind of life?" she thought.

Panicking at the thought, Grace suddenly screamed out, "No! Stop it! Take your hands off me!"

She screamed so loud that both the taxi driver and Ron were shocked. She took advantage of the confusion, screamed at the driver to pull over, and rushed out of the taxi before Ron could react. She ran like there was no tomorrow. She ran and ran for what seemed like forever. But as the adrenaline wore off, Grace suddenly found herself out of breath, angry and no idea where she was. She was not familiar with this city and it was getting late. She managed to find a pay phone in a gas station, dialed the hotel number, and asked the operator to locate Daniel.

By the time the operator was able to get Daniel on the phone, Grace could hardly speak she was trembling so badly, "Hey, Daniel...."

"Grace, what happened? Where are you? Are you okay?" Daniel asked.

Grace found she couldn't function very well, but told him, "I am okay, but I need help, Daniel. I am not sure where I am at."

"Where is Ron? Weren't you guys together?" Daniel asked with concern in his voice.

"We were, but not any more. I will explain it all to you later, but would you mind coming to pick me up?" Grace felt herself almost begging him to rescue her.

"Sure, tell me what you see around you," Daniel said, eager to get her back to safety.

When Daniel finally got to the gas station where she had sought refuge, Grace couldn't hold herself in check any longer. She burst into tears as she ran to Daniel.

"Did he touch you?" Daniel asked with his thick and low voice.

"Almost, but I ran off," Grace answered, still sobbing uncontrollably.

Daniel looked at her with sympathetic, caring eyes and declared, "I'll make sure it never happens again."

Ask Yourself

- If you were Grace, what would be your reaction when John came to visit you?

- Why do you think Grace was attracted to Daniel?

- Can you tell what was going on in Grace's mind when Ron was about to take advantage of her? What would you have done?

Chapter 4

Tasting the Goodness

T he following day's sales presentation was a success. Grace kept her distance from Ron. Ron was acting like nothing had happened, so did Grace. In the culture Grace lived in, she felt there was no use in bringing up the incident. She couldn't fight against Ron and felt people would most likely perceive it was Graces' fault or she was trying to "sleep with boss" in order to get a promotion. The team returned to Taipei without further incident and Grace just wanted to put it all behind her.

After a long tiring week, Grace was especially looking forward to the weekend. When she arrived at work Friday morning, she was surprised to find a note and a rose on her desk. Curious, she quickly set her things down and hurried towards her desk. After carefully unfolding the note, she read, "Will you go to dinner with me tonight?" It was signed with a cursive "D." Grace's heart leapt as she read it. She quickly got a vase and some water and carefully placed the rose in it. The rest of the morning Grace was in ecstasy. During her lunch break, she went to find Daniel, certain the note was from him. After only a few moments of looking, she found him.

"I take it you got my note," he said with a smile.

"Yes," Grace replied blushing.

"Well…?" Daniel asked.

"Of course I'll go out with you!" she said excitedly.

"Excellent!" Daniel responded, "We'll leave right after work."

Grace couldn't wait to get off of work that evening. It was Friday, she'd met her quota of sales for the month already, and she was about to go on her first date! Could things get any better?

To Grace's amazement, things did get better. Very soon after that first date, Daniel asked Grace to be his girlfriend. Eagerly she consented. Now it was time for her to be introduced to his family. Daniel was the youngest of four children and the only son. Nobody in his family approved of them dating because of the eight-year difference in their ages, except his father. Though a tough and hard-to-please man, Daniel's father took a liking to Grace. They shared a connection that Grace did not fully understand, but was grateful for. They had a strong bond which Grace was very sorrowful to lose when a few months later Daniel's father passed away. Grace had felt Daniel's father had been her protection from the rest of the family and felt very unwelcomed around them after he was gone. She was the subject of scorn as Daniel's three older sisters obviously looked down on her.

Despite his family's negative opinion of her, Daniel soon proposed to Grace. Grace had a deep desire to leave her mother's home. She wanted to be independent. She was also very lonely and Daniel made her feel loved and wanted. Growing up without a father, Grace also longed to have someone to look out for her and protect her. She felt in her gut marrying Daniel was not the right thing for her, but her needs were so strong that she accepted his proposal regardless of her inner reservations. Though it didn't feel quite right, it made Grace happy to think that she would soon be getting married. She thought about it all the time, except when she was at school. There, she was always extremely focused.

A Christian University

Grace enjoyed school very much and when she was there, she felt renewed. Regardless the stress of the week, when she was at school she felt invigorated as she eagerly fed her hunger for knowledge and passion for learning. She majored in Japanese and minored in English. She wanted to earn two degrees.

The university she attended was a Christian university. Grace was always invited to go to the daily chapel meetings, but never did thinking it was unimportant and uninteresting. There were times though when she was tempted to go in just to listen to the songs they sang. Grace had always had a love for singing and had sung in the choir all throughout school. During junior high school, she also played the xylophone in the orchestra which was number one in the nation. Noticing they were looking for choir members, Grace auditioned and was selected to be in the university choir. She enjoyed it and loved learning about music. They often sang Christian hymns, but Grace had no idea the songs she was singing were Christian, nor did she have an understanding of what they meant.

Grace didn't know why, but at this university she felt something she had not felt anywhere else or at any other time in her life, except once. She remembered when she was younger they had an elderly couple as neighbors, who would invite Grace and her brother to their home every afternoon to have a cookie. They had a picture of Jesus at the last supper hanging on their wall. Grace never knew what it was, but she got a warm feeling when she looked at it. The couple were very kind and Grace felt safe and loved when she was at their home. However, their customs seemed very strange to the children. Each afternoon before they ate their cookies, the couple would bow their heads and pray to someone they called Father God. Grace wondered who God was and why they called Him their Father. She remembered she and Michael had simply followed along as the couple prayed.

Thinking back to her own home, Grace remembered how her mother had always worshiped many different idols, as well as participating in the cultural tradition of worshipping the family's ancestors. As a child Grace had thought perhaps that was who this couple had been praying to—their father. Grace had never liked being made to worship with her mother. It never gave their family any peace. Yet Grace had definitely experience peace in that couple's home when they had prayed to their, "Father God." Grace wanted to feel that peace all the time, even as a child but always felt it was not her place to ask. Upon remembering this, many questions came to Grace's mind. Was what she was feeling here at the university the same as what she had felt in that elderly couple's home as a child? She suddenly longed to feel that warmth and love wherever she went. She certainly felt it very strongly here at school, especially in choir. Choir made her happy and gave her a drive to excel.

Apparently Grace was not the only one driven to succeed. Her university's choir got into the national competition every year and had a reputation for winning. Her instructor had graduated from the renowned, Juilliard School of Music, so consequently demanded excellence from the students. Their excellence gave them an opportunity to perform at the national opera house where Grace was chosen to perform a solo. She was overcome with amazement. She had never performed a solo before and especially not in front of thousands of people. Grace was to sing a Christian song, though she did not understand its words.

When the day of the performance arrived, Grace nervously waited to sing her solo. She hoped that she would not forget the words. She often heard her professors speak of Jesus, though she did not understand who He was. All she knew was that He was someone they prayed to and their prayers seemed to work, so she decided to utter a little prayer of her own.

"Jesus, whoever You are, please help me to do good today. Help me to remember all my words and hit all my notes. That's all I guess...thanks."

Moments later, Grace was up. As she sang her first note, she felt all her nervousness leave and immediately replaced by a calm confidence. At the end of the solo all the crowd cheered and her instructor gave her a nod of approval. As the song ended Grace said a quiet, "Thank you" to this Jesus who had answered her prayer.

Though Jesus was often spoken of at the university, Grace always thought of Him as a western man because His name did not make sense in Chinese translation. Christians understood what it meant because they were constantly taught about Him, but Grace was not a Christian so it made no sense to her. She wondered why she had not heard of Jesus before she entered the university because, ironically, Taiwan was founded on Christianity. How could someone who is so important to Christians be so seldom spoken of in a Christian area like Taiwan?

Ask Yourself

- Has anyone ever shown you the goodness of God? If yes, in what way?
- Can you relate to Grace's desire to marry Daniel? What are the triggers caused her to feel this way?
- What kind of breakthrough did Grace have when she went to sing a solo in front of the multitude?

Chapter 5

Escaping into a "Marriage Refuge"

G race spent four blissful years at the university. During the last two years she was engaged to be married to Daniel. After graduating from the university, Grace began to make wedding plans. She was very excited and couldn't wait for the day to come. Grace had everything planned out down to the smallest detail. She wanted her wedding day to be perfect.

The Funeral

One afternoon as Grace was busily occupied with wedding preparations, a very emotional Anne walked into her room and said, "Grace, I need to tell you something."

"Sure, what's going on, mom?" Grace asked, thinking it was probably the pre-wedding syndrome of a parent and quickly played some scripts in her head as to how to comfort Anne.

Before Grace could say anything further, Anne said in a barely audible voice, "Your father just passed away."

Grace stopped what she was doing and stared at the floor as she waited for her mother to continue.

"Grace, I need you and Michael to attend the funeral for me," Anne said as she finally broke the silence.

Without a moment's hesitation Grace replied, "I don't think so!"

"Come on, Grace, please," Anne pleaded, "After all, he was your father."

Grace couldn't contain the rage roaring from deep inside of her as she angrily responded, "And exactly what made him a father? Was it his sperm, broken promises, and his countless mistresses?"

"Grace, please! You need to show some respect to him and the other family members," Anne cautioned.

"What family members?" Grace asked, totally surprised at her mother's mindset. "Do you seriously think Michael and I should get together with all his other mistresses' and their children, and have a party? Maybe we could all complain about how he put us all in misery?!"

"I just need you to show your face at the funeral on my behalf, Grace," her mother insisted, "There will be no further discussion about this!"

"Besides, I am the one that should be complaining, not you," Anne said as she turned and walked out of Grace's room, leaving her feeling totally helpless and alone.

Since Michael refused to attend the funeral, Grace was alone on the domestic flight to Western Taiwan. When she arrived at the airport "Aunt" Cindy, whom she had never met, came to pick her up.

"You must be Grace," Cindy said holding up a sign with Grace's name on it.

"Yes, I am," Grace replied trying to squeeze out some sort of a smile.

"I am so glad you are here. John would be very happy to know you were here," Cindy commented as they walked towards the parking lot.

Grace couldn't help herself as she responded, "I don't think so, since he didn't care much about his daughters when he was alive."

"I know, Grace," Cindy nodded, "but after all, he gave you life."

Grace clamped her mouth shut as her mind screamed, "No, he didn't give me life, he gave us all hell!"

The next three days were like an eternity for Grace as she met many other "brothers and sisters" that were all strangers to her. She could not shed a tear during the funeral as her mind focused only on the "hatred" she felt towards John. There was nothing else left inside of her for this man who had biologically but never physically fathered her. She just wanted it over and done with so she could get back to her wedding preparations.

The Marriage Refuge

After several months of careful planning and arranging, her big day was finally upon her. Grace was nervous as she slipped into the white dress she had bought from a nearby boutique. It was simple, yet elegant. Grace stared at herself in the mirror as the bridesmaids placed the veil on her head. She couldn't believe that today was the day she had been dreaming of! It was time for the bridal procession to make their way to the ceremony. The wedding was being held in a small pagoda by a waterfall. When Grace arrived, she saw everyone seated and awaiting her entrance. The music began to play and all eyes were on her as she made her way to the groom. "I can't believe I'm finally doing this!" she thought. When Grace reached Daniel, they turned to face the priest and the ceremony began. The wedding was beautiful, just as Grace had imagined it. The thought of starting their new life together excited Grace. She knew it wouldn't always be easy, but she was ready for the adventure—or so she thought.

Grace loved having someone to come home to every night and she especially loved not living with her mother. But for some reason, despite all her efforts, Grace had a difficult time assuming her role as a wife. She had a constant sense that something wasn't right, but she ignored it. As the years progressed, being married became harder and harder for Grace.

During the fifth year of their marriage, Grace noticed that Daniel had begun acting very strange. He wasn't himself anymore. He invested into some risky business opportunity and lost a great deal of money. It surely didn't help much as he hardly communicated with Grace. He probably thought Grace was too young to understand. Grace and Daniel treated each other like strangers. They had hard time to squeeze out any meaningful conversation. Daniel started coming home late with heavy smell of alcohol which reminded Grace about Anne and Jo's lifestyle.

This worried Grace, but she wished it would pass. However, the longer she waited, the worse it got. He was often very verbally abusive to Grace and she could not understand what had caused him to take such a sudden, drastic turn for the worse. Going into their sixth year of marriage, Grace realized that it was almost not possible to talk to Daniel without raising up voice or feeling to be put down like a failure! One day when Daniel was yelling at Grace, Grace decided she'd had enough.

"I want a divorce!" she exclaimed over his shouting.

Immediately Daniel stopped yelling and asked, "What did you say?"

"You heard me. I'm tired of you treating me however you want and not being able to do anything about it," Grace said as tears trickled down her face. "You don't love me anymore. We need to get a divorce."

"That's not true!" Daniel argue, "I do love you. You know that."

"I know you used to love me," Grace admitted, "but you're not the same man I married six years ago. Something's not right with our relationship, Daniel. I can't keep living like this and we even cannot talk to each other like normal people, there's nothing left for me to do except walk away from this marriage."

As she turned to walk away, Daniel grabbed her arm and cried, "No! I won't let you just give up on us! You can't!"

Grace pulled away from him and slowly backed out of the room as she told him, "You gave up on us a long time ago."

As Grace and her husband were in the process of getting the divorce, she began looking for another job. Many of her university classmates had gone to work for large Japanese corporations as secretaries. They were good jobs with good pay, provided a sense of security for these young women, except there was no advancement of it. But Grace was not pleased with the thought of serving men just as every other woman did. "I didn't work this hard for this long just to have Japanese men order me around," she thought.

She saw an ad for a job at The W Hotel. Grace knew it had been built next to the convention center which attracted many people in the summer time. "This looks interesting," Grace said to herself and decided to pursue it. She went to her first interview on a hot Wednesday afternoon. She wore shorts and a tank top with no makeup on. Her outfit was similar to what she had worn for her last job interview.

When she opened the hotel doors and started to go into the interviewing room, she froze. Everyone in the room was in business attire—everyone except her. She quickly backed out of the room and closed the door, hoping no one had seen her. She leaned against the wall as she debated with herself about what to do.

"I can't go back in there. But I have to. But everyone will make fun of me. When the employer sees how casual I'm dressed, he'll think I don't take this seriously and I won't get the job. Should I go change? No I don't have time. It's too late to go back now."

As Grace muttered to herself, she didn't notice the man who had come up and was now standing next to her.

"Who are you talking to?" he asked with a smile.

Grace quickly looked up realizing she must have spoken out loud.

"Huh? Oh, no one," she said smiling sheepishly back at him.

"Are you here for the interview?" the man asked seemingly unaware of her discomfort.

"Yes. I suppose I am," she replied as she glanced once more at her unprofessional outfit.

The man chuckled, "Well, we'd better get in there then. It should be starting any minute."

He held the door open for Grace as they both entered the room. She felt so out of place. It seemed that everyone was staring at her. She quickly seated herself by the man she'd met outside the door. She didn't know him, but he seemed friendly and at least he wouldn't judge her based on what she was wearing. A hush came over everyone as the interviewer walked in. She was carrying a large clipboard and Grace thought she looked extremely stern. Grace felt a bit intimidated and immediately sat up straighter in her chair as if she had been reprimanded by a teacher. Everyone watched as the woman made her way to the center of the room.

"Thank you all for coming," she said in a commanding tone. "We will be doing individual interviews today, so when I call your name you will follow me into the adjacent room," she motioned towards a door on the right, "and the interview will begin. We will ask you a series of questions. Please answer completely and specifically. Are there any questions?" She looked around the room and finding nobody with a question simply said, "Then we shall begin."

She called the first name and began the interviews. Grace waited for just over forty-five minutes as the room slowly emptied. She was the last one and couldn't wait to get it over with. After a few moments, the door opened and the woman emerged and called Grace's name. Grace stood and walked toward the woman. The woman eyed Grace's attire, sighed heavily and led her into the room. Grace took a seat across from the woman. The woman began to ask questions which Grace answered as best she could.

The interview lasted about twenty minutes, then the woman stood and opened the door for Grace indicating the interview was over. Grace felt confident in the answers she had given and she could tell the woman was impressed with them. Before leaving, Grace turned to shake the woman's hand.

"Thank you for coming," the woman said, "someone will be in touch with you shortly."

"Thank you," Grace replied, "I look forward to hearing from you."

As Grace turned to walk away, the woman stopped her and said with obvious distain, "If you get called to come back, do not wear those clothes again."

All Grace could do was nod and reply with a respectful, "Yes, Ma'am."

December the eighth, Grace's divorce was finalized and she moved back in with her mother. The date of the divorce was the same day Grace and Daniel had married seven years ago. Daniel intentionally chose that day because he wanted her to remember it forever—the day now reflected only sorrow for her!

A short time later, Grace was surprised to receive a phone call from the hotel asking her to come back for another interview. Grace happily returned to the hotel, this time in proper business attire. Several days later, she was called back for yet another interview. She went to a total of five interviews before finally getting hired as a telephone operator at the hotel. Excited, she went to call her mother. When Anne picked up the phone, Grace shared the good news.

"Guess what!" she happily exclaimed, "I got the job!"

"Doing what?" asked Anne.

"I will be a telephone operator at The W Hotel," Grace responded enthusiastically.

"What! A telephone operator?" her mother shouted into the phone, "You went through all those years of school just to becoming a telephone operator? I thought you were going to get a good job!"

"This is a good job," Grace explained, "I know it doesn't seem like much now, but I'll work my way up. Besides, the pay is good and I think I could learn a lot here."

A New Life—A New Career

And learn she did. On top of having to manage 150 lines and remember 500 extensions, Grace was also trained in the other hotel departments as well. Grace liked this system because it meant that everyone was able to work anywhere in the hotel if the manager wanted them to. They all knew how to do everything in each department. Grace was promoted very soon after she started at The W Hotel just as she had told her mother she would. She was a very hard worker and worked her way up to become the manager of sales. Due to her promotion to the managerial position, she met the engineering director, Frank. He taught Grace many useful techniques at the hotel and the two quickly became good friends.

One day, Frank brought Grace to a small Christian bookstore with him. Grace had never been in a Christian bookstore before, but from the moment she walked in the door she felt that same warm feeling she had felt at the elderly couple's house when she was younger and at the university. Soft Christian music was playing in the background and Grace tried to listen to the lyrics. As she listened to, "More love, more power, more of you in my life," Grace wondered who the "you" was that the singer wanted in their life.

Grace browsed around and scanned the book titles as she walked through the store waiting for Frank to make his purchase. She stopped when she saw a book entitled, "Streams in the Desert." It was labeled as a devotional. Grace was intrigued by the title and decided to purchase the book. She left the store with Frank feeling very happy, though she did not understand why. Grace read the devotional everyday even though she did not own a Bible and could not understand the scripture references.

Shortly after their visit to the Christian bookstore, Frank called Grace and invited her to go to church with him the next morning. Remembering how the last place she went with him had such a positive effect on her, Grace agreed. She met Frank the next morning in the parking lot of a small church called, "The Oasis." It was an international church and the pastors, Scott and Jenny, were Americans. Chinese churches were difficult to find at that time, so Grace had never really been to church before. Daniel had taken her to a Buddhist temple with him once before, but Grace did not enjoy that at all. She didn't quite know what to expect this time and wondered if she would like it.

To her great surprise, she did enjoy it very much. It was exactly what Grace had been looking for; a place to learn about Jesus and experience all the love she had so desperately longed for in her life. Grace began attending church regularly and became close with the pastor and his wife. She also attended what they called cell groups, where a small group of people would meet and have a Bible study. Grace's cell group met on Tuesday nights and Grace looked forward to it every week. Even though she did not fully understand the Bible, she read it consistently and began to understand more of it as time passed.

A New Found Faith

Grace was not yet baptized, but understood the importance of it. She was waiting for the right time. After church one Sunday, her pastor asked her if she would join them at a worship concert/conference that week. Thinking it was just a concert, Grace agreed. To her amazement, it was more than just a concert. It was a time of pure worship to God. Sitting on the front row with her pastors, Grace felt God's presence closer than she ever had before. It was almost tangible.

The conference lasted three days and Grace enjoyed every moment of it. On the final day, the worship leader called the audience down to the stage. Everyone stood as close to the grand piano which he was playing as they could. He then began to pray for everyone. During this time, Grace's eyes felt very heavy. "Don't fall into sleep!" she kept telling herself. But it was no use, within moments Grace had passed out on the floor. Lying there, she saw a series of movie frames. In the first frame, she saw a gooey substance like honey in her palms, in the second frame, it began to drip down to the ground, and then lastly it lit up the surrounding area.

When Grace awoke, she was on the ground and Pastor Scott and another man were standing over her. They helped her up and back to her seat. Her pastor then asked her what she had seen. "How does he know I saw something?" she thought. She then relayed to him what she had seen. She had no idea what her vision meant and was still amazed at how it even happened.

At the end of the conference, the event organizer came up and thanked everyone for coming and pointed out banners that read, "Enjoy His Presence," "Take Up His Mission," and "Deliver the Healing Oil to the Nations." When she read this, Grace knew that was the meaning of what she had seen. She also determined she needed to get baptized very soon and spoke with Pastor Scott about it. The next available church baptism date was December 8. Grace had a business trip planned to Japan but would return on the seventh, so she made plans to be baptized on the eighth.

When Grace was driving to church the week before she left for the business meeting, she narrowly avoided a fatal car accident. Out of nowhere, one car came at her from the right, and another from the left. Panicked, Grace sped up to avoid the collision. The cars barely missed her as they crashed into each other. Shaken, Grace tried to refocus on the road, but suddenly heard a voice.

"I will kill you!" it shouted.

Grace did not know where it had come from. There was nobody else in the car with her. This frightened her and upon arriving at church, she hurried to get inside where she knew she was safe. After service, she did not hesitate to find her pastor and tell him what had happened. Alarmed, Scott called his wife over and they immediately began to pray over Grace.

When Grace arrived in Japan for the business meeting, she was informed that the Japanese had changed the schedule to where Grace would not be able to get home until late afternoon on December 8. Upon hearing this, Grace's heart sank. Her baptism was scheduled for the morning of December 8! She sat in her hotel room feeling distressed. Then she remembered the song she had heard in the bookstore; "More love, more power, more of You in my life." Grace softly sang the words to herself, suddenly realizing that the singer was talking about God.

"I do need more of You in my life," she said as she looked up toward the ceiling. "But I'm never going to have more of You unless I can do this. I need to be baptized."

She called her pastor and explained the situation to him.

"Well, Grace," Scott said, "I know how much you want to do this, and I think it's very important. Tell you what, when you get back from

Japan, no matter what time you arrive, just give me a call. Jenny and I will come over and have a baptism for you there in your home."

Overjoyed Grace replied, "Thank you so much, Pastor! That means so much to me. I really feel I need to be baptized on the eighth!"

"I know," Scott affirmed, "So don't worry about getting back in time. We'll do it when you do get back. Just give us a call when you get situated."

Grace thanked her pastor once more then hung up the phone. She thanked God for working things out so she could still be baptized on the eighth of December.

Grace awoke on December 8th and the same song came to her mind again. The entire day she couldn't get the song out of her head. She knew she had to call Pastor Scott as soon as she got home. She needed to be baptized that night! When she finally arrived at her apartment, she immediately went to the phone. She called her pastor saying she wanted to be baptized that day. Her mother, who had overheard the phone call, came and leaned against the counter next to Grace.

"Who was that?" she asked.

"My pastor," said Grace. "He and his wife are coming over later to baptize me."

"Baptize you? Why on earth would you want to be baptized?" her mother asked.

"So I can dedicate myself to God," Grace explained.

"God? We have many gods, Grace," Anne reminded her. "None is greater than the other. You should not commit yourself to just one god."

"But He's the only One there is," Grace told her mother.

"Nonsense!" Anne scoffed, "What's gotten into you? Who's this "God" they're teaching you about over at that church of yours?"

"The only true God there is," Grace said with conviction, "The One who created the whole world and all the people and animals and everything we see in nature."

"Indeed! I must say I'm surprised that you've even taken an interest in such an outlandish doctrine. But do what you want, Grace. Just know that I think this whole baptism thing is completely absurd," Anne said as she left the room.

Grace did not care about her mother's opinions. She knew Anne would not approve, but she hoped that one day she could convince her mother to at least come to church with her. It was 8:45 p.m. when Grace heard a knock at the door. She eagerly answered it and saw not only her pastors, but her entire cell group as well. She was so happy that they had all come. They went out to the complex's pool where Grace was to be baptized. After she had repeated after the pastor and made a commitment to God in front of everyone, she was dunked under the water. When she came up she began to cry. She tried her hardest to stop but could not.

She heard God say to her, "Today you are My bride."

That was the first time Grace had clearly heard God's voice. She was overwhelmed with joy. Up until now Grace had hated this day because December 8 was a constant reminder of her former relationship with Daniel, who purposely picked that date to marry and then divorce her.

Now she would remember it as the wedding between her and Christ. Grace went and told her mother that she would no longer worship idols with her.

"What do you mean?" Anne asked, shocked by what Grace had just told her.

"I mean I will only worship the one true God whom I serve. No more idols. No more worshiping ancestors," Grace said knowing God was with her, "They can't do anything for us."

"You mean when I die, you won't worship me?" her mother asked.

"No, Mother. I'm sorry," Grace said firmly, "I don't believe in that and to be honest I never really have."

"You don't believe in it anymore? I'm disappointed in you, Grace," her mother said to her shaking her head sadly, "I've raised you better than this."

"Mother, I truly appreciate what you have done for me and Michael. I know you have tried your best to raise us up," Grace affirmed, "but whether you noticed it or not, you have also raised me to be on my own. That's how it's always been. I was always alone. I've learned to think and do for myself. I have gotten to where I am without any help from you. You raised me to be independent, which I am and have been for years. You have hardly listened to me and never taken any real interest in my life. Ever since I was little all I wanted was to make you proud, but nothing I did was ever good enough for you! I'm done trying to please you. I'm living my life now and I'll choose to believe whatever I want to believe. Sorry I'm such a disappointment to you, but I guess that's how it's always been, right?"

Anne was outraged by the time Grace finished her speech, "How dare you speak to me like that! You never would have spoken this way to your grandmother. You always liked her better."

"At least she spent time with Michael and me. At least we knew she cared," Grace countered, "You were never there for us, especially after you started dating Jo. Things between you two have only gotten worse and yet you still stay with him. You obviously don't know what's best for you, or for this family."

"And I suppose you do?" Anne asked sarcastically.

"No," Grace admitted, "But if you can't take care of yourself then you clearly can't take care of anyone else. Grandmother was always the one who took care of us, but then she got Alzheimer and I've been taking care of myself ever since."

"Well she's gone now, and your marriage ended in disaster," Anne reminded her, "So Michael and I are all you've got."

"Yes, but that doesn't mean I'm going to continue living your lifestyle. All it's brought me is a whole lot of confusion," Grace declared, "and I'm done with it!"

Anne crossed her arms and sighed heavily, "Fine. You're a woman. Make your own decisions. It's clear you have been for a while now. But you've been worshiping with me for years, why stop now?"

"Because I don't believe in the same things you do," Grace tried once again to explain. "I refuse to worship someone who is not real."

"If you won't even pray to your own ancestors, then you dishonor your family," Anne warned her.

"So be it," said Grace obstinately.

"I see. Well if that is what you choose, then your loyalties are no longer to this family," Anne said angrily, "You are no longer my daughter!"

Anne stormed off, leaving Grace standing in the center of the room. Was this really happening? Had her mother just disowned her? Where would she go now? What would she do? Wasn't committing her life to God supposed to make things easier?

Ask Yourself

- What are your thoughts about Grace's reaction to John's death?
- Do you believe there is a spiritual realm existing of both the Dark and the Light?
- Have you tried to follow God, but in the process found that instead of things getting easier, it got harder for you?

Chapter 6

Starting a New Life

G od began to deal with Grace through the Scriptures during her daily devotion time telling her it was time for her to move out. When she read, *"Leave Babylon, flee from the Babylonians! Announce this with shouts of joy and proclaim it"* (Isaiah 48:20), Grace sensed God nudging her to take action fast! She wanted to move out and knew she needed to but felt she couldn't afford it.

She told God, "Lord, that's easy to say but I don't have the money."

He replied to her heart, "Look for a place first."

Grace was scared, but did as God had commanded. She spent several weeks looking for an apartment. When she finally found one she liked, the landlord told her the rental was nearly USD$600 dollars a month and a two-month security deposit was required before she could move in. She told God she did not have the money for that apartment, although she knew it was the one.

The next morning during her devotion time, the words in the Bible seemed to jump off the page for her. First she read 2 Corinthians 12:9.

But he said to me, "My grace is sufficient for you, for my power is made perfect in weakness." Therefore I will boast all the more gladly about my weaknesses, so that Christ's power may rest on me."

Then she read the story of Abraham and how he had faith in God's provision and later become one of the wealthiest men of his time. Abraham believed and then he acted on that belief

"God will provide a sheep for the burnt offering, my son," Abraham answered. And they both walked on together."(Genesis 22:8)

While Grace was believing for God's provision to come in for her apartment, she received word that she had been transferred to another department at work with a schedule which left her unable to attend church on Sundays. Grace was part of the worship team leadership, so she needed to be there. Plus church was the only thing that kept her going throughout the week. She couldn't miss it. She knew her spiritual life would suffer without it. This confirmed to Grace that the "Get Out of Babylon" message from God was not just about moving out from her mother's place, but also to quit her job! But how on earth could she afford to rent the place she liked while at the same time have no clue as to where her next job was to be?

Grace started preparing and sending out resumes where she felt God was leading her and thought to herself, "I'd better find a new job before I resign from my current job." The next few days, wherever Grace turned the same verses would come to her through people, magazines and songs. Grace knew it was God again telling her she needed to leave her job and get out of her mother's house. God always spoke very directly to Grace. She knew it was Him. The only struggle she was having was she had not had one job interview yet. Grace was reminded about Abraham's story and that he stepped out by faith first, then God's provision showed up.

God's Provision

Grace submitted her resignation letter the next day. Though she was still without another job, she had an unspeakable peace in her heart. Her general manager, Tom had treated Grace as his own daughter and was very confused and upset when he found her letter of resignation on his desk.

"Did you get another job?" he asked as he glanced at her letter of resignation sitting on the desk before him.

"No, Boss," Grace calmly replied.

Tom looked skeptical saying, "You know, Grace, you can tell me if you've gone to work for one of our competitors."

"No," she quickly said shaking her head, "I'm going to go somewhere else but I just don't know where yet."

"I don't understand," her general manager said, "Why would you quit a good job when you don't even have another one?"

Grace was quiet for a moment, then began slowly to try and explain, "Because, my God told me to."

"Your God?" he asked, "Grace, I know you're into this new faith and all, but don't let this superstition stuff guide you the wrong way."

"Look, Boss," Grace said trying to reassure him, "I can't explain it but I know I have to do this."

In Grace's mind she felt like she was doing the wrong thing, but in her heart she knew it was right. She told him she felt she needed to work in a bank. He scoffed as he reminded her that she did not have a degree in finance.

"What are you thinking?!" he asked with a hint of disbelief in his voice.

"All I know is that I just need to do it," Grace told him firmly.

"Have you sent in a resume to any banks?" he asked really wanting to help her.

"Yes," Grace told him.

"Which one?" he asked, "Is it the local bank?"

"No," Grace replied, "the Universal Bank."

The Universal Bank was the most prestigious bank in Taiwan. Her boss felt that Grace was too inexperienced to work there. He was certain they would not accept her.

"Why there?" he asked hoping once again to change her mind about leaving.

"I don't really know," she admitted, "They're looking for someone to do marketing so I sent in my resume."

After a few more attempts to try to get Grace to change her mind, Grace's boss let her go with three months' compensation. He had never done that for anyone else. When Grace left his office she felt joy and a sense of release. She let out a long sigh of relief as she walked out of the building. She was deeply touched at her boss's generous gesture. With that settled and done, all Grace had to do now was to go home and wait.

Less than two months after Grace's resignation, Universal Bank called Grace in for an interview! Grace was totally thrilled and nervous all at once! At that time, if you were working at the international bank, your social status was perceived as "upper class." Grace had been told that the interview process generally took up to a month with multiple meetings before one would know the outcome.

When Grace arrived at the bank, she got out of her car, and gazed up at the tall building. It was a bit daunting so as she made her way into the building, and entered one of the elevators, she talked to God. She knew this was big.

"Lord, this is the Universal Bank," she said, "I'm going to go up to the eleventh floor for this interview. I don't know if I can even survive here, but if this is Your will, I pray that they will offer me the job at NT$85,000 a month, so I can afford the apartment You've shown me. Thank you, Lord."

Suddenly realizing that without a parking space in the city of Taiwan, Grace would have to pay a large parking fee, she quickly added, "Oh, by the way, I will need them to supply a parking space for me, too, Lord. Thank you."

When she arrived on the eleventh, she was met by an elegantly-dressed lady who brought her into a small lounge and motioned for Grace to sit.

"Grace, I'll let Ms. Chen know you have arrived," she said graciously, "please excuse me for a moment."

Alone in the lounge, Grace took time to observe her surroundings thinking, "Bank environment is surely very different; neat and high-end but sort of cold and impersonal."

A few moments later, the lady was back and guided Grace into a beautiful office. The door sign said, "Ms. Nancy Chen, Vice President."

Grace entered the office with her heart beating at double its normal speed and was instructed to take the seat across the desk from Ms. Chen, who wasted no time getting to the point. She started to ask Grace a series of marketing related questions. Grace felt Ms. Chen was pleased with Grace's answers.

Thirty minutes later Ms. Chen said, "Grace we are going to do something we have never done before. We looked at your resume, did our research, and we think you are the perfect candidate for this brand new position in our department. Here is the offer letter."

Grace's heart stopped! First of all, though she had prayed, she hadn't seen it coming this fast. Then, as she glanced through the offer which was printed on premium grade stationary, the salary was exactly what she had asked God for, plus she was being given a parking space! "What's going on, am I dreaming or is this for real?" Grace thought to herself as she tried to comprehend what had just happened.

Due to Grace's silence, Ms. Chen asked, "Is that not enough?"

Grace quietly but eagerly accepted the offer. She couldn't believe God had given her exactly what she'd asked for! After she left the building, she immediately went to the pay phone to call Tom, her former boss.

"I got a job!" she exclaimed as he answered the phone.

"That's great!" he said excitedly, "Where at?"

"Mr. Tom, it's at the Universal Bank!" Grace said breathlessly.

"What?" Tom asked, totally surprised by her answer

Grace explained how they had created a position just for her because they did not have a marketing department for credit cards.

"That's in-cre-di-ble," Tom admitted, "Maybe this faith thing of yours really does work. Congratulations!"

Now that Grace had the job she needed, she knew she had to move out of her mother's apartment. The day arrived and Pastor Scott and two other men from the church came to help Grace out. When Pastor Scott stepped into Grace's room, he was amazed at how much she had managed to pack up and move around to have things ready for them.

"Did you do all of this by yourself?" He asked with compassion, knowing things had not been easy for Grace.

"Yes, Pastor" Grace replied sadly, "I didn't have much choice."

As they were moving boxes out of the apartment, Anne sat playing mahjong at the table with three men Grace did not know. She didn't even look up or speak a word to Grace. As they were moving the final box out of the apartment, one of the men at the table with Anne mockingly asked Pastor Scott if he wanted to gamble with them.

When Pastor Scott politely declined, the man laughed, "But I thought your Jesus loved to be with sinners like us?"

It was one thing to ridicule her faith, but it was like a knife in Grace's heart when they mocked her pastor and her Lord. She was indeed leaving Babylon behind.

Ask Yourself

- Do you take the words in the Bible literally the way Grace did in this chapter?

- Why do you think Grace had the faith to do what God asked her to?

- Have you ever been "disowned" or cast out by your family? Why do you think God allowed it to happen to Grace?

Chapter 7

Testing What I Am Made Of

T hree months after Grace had begun her new job and settled into her new apartment, she got a call from her brother saying that Anne was gone. Michael relayed that she had left a note saying, "Don't try to find me, I have no desire to live." Grace hurried to Anne's apartment, and found out Anne had taken none of her belongings; not even underwear or ID. Alarmed by this, Grace and Michael started searching for their mother. As they widened their search, Grace also discovered that Anne had taken off with all of Grace's savings.

Anne's gambling addiction had gotten her deeply in debt, which Grace thought was most likely the reason for her disappearance. She hadn't paid the rent in two months and it was due again in a week. Michael had to move in with a friend. He and Grace cleared out the apartment so they could return it to the landlord. He had given them a week to move out. They needed to get rid of all the furniture. Since neither she nor Michael had space for it, Grace decided to sell it all to get her brother some money to live on so he could get on with his life as well. She posted the list in her church bulletin, as she continued to pray for all of them!

With only four days left before the landlord would reclaim the apartment, Grace tiredly went there to sort more things out and pray for a solution. After a long day of working in the bank, she was not looking forward to an evening sorting through her mother's things. She was pleasantly surprised when she met a wonderful Christian couple who had just moved in next door. At the time, only about 2% of the population were Christians, so to meet one right next door was a miracle in itself! They felt an instant bond and Grace felt God was showing her that she was not alone in all of this. The couple offered to post the list of furniture in their church bulletin as well.

After another two days passed with no further progress in selling their belongings, Grace received a phone call from a lady who expressed an interest in her listing. As Grace went to meet her at the apartment after work that evening, she prayed, "Lord, please let her at least buy something, the cooking pans, some chairs—something!"

At first it appeared the lady was not interested in anything and then she suddenly broke the silence asking, "Is everything for sale?"

"Yes," Grace nodded hopefully, "Have you found anything you like?"

Grace expected the woman to choose one or two items since she still seemed to be totally uninterested.

"I'd like to buy everything," said the woman with a smile.

Grace was shocked and asked what she felt must have been the stupidest question ever, "Everything! Do you mean everything?"

"That's right. You see my son is getting married," the woman said with an even bigger smile on her face. "He and his fiancé are going to need things for their new home so your items here are saving me quite a bit of time and money."

"Well, that's wonderful! Congratulations, that's great!" Grace managed to say, trying to figure out what just happened. "However, I am running out of time to empty out this apartment so could you arrange to pick everything up by tomorrow evening? I know it's not a reasonable request, but..."

Before she could finish her request, the woman interrupted her saying, "Oh, that's not a problem at all. In fact, I'd like to take it all today if that's alright. I have two workers outside with a truck ready to load everything. I believe you can see them from the balcony."

Grace went to the balcony and looked out to see a large moving truck parked right beneath the apartment building. She was amazed and speechless to say the least! Most people took public transportation in this highly populated area so for this woman to say she had a truck waiting was another kind of miracle!

"I can pay in cash," the woman said surprising the already dumbfounded Grace.

Fumbling for words, Grace managed to convey her acceptance of the woman's generous offer. Her eyes were wide as her confusion quickly turned to a smile, and then to a grin. She couldn't believe it. "Is this woman an angel?" Grace thought.

"If I may ask," Grace began, "what do you do for a living?"

"Oh, my husband and I are farmers. We transport fresh produce to the city everyday," she replied. "That is why I have the truck and the workers on hand."

Grace was still trying to understand it all as the workman make quick work of packing up and loading everything left in the apartment into the woman's truck. Watching them drive away, Grace was astounded. She looked up to the sky and uttered a big, "Thank You!" The apartment situation had been taken care of, but there was still no sign of their missing mother.

Guilt, Shame, Blame

The search for Anne continued and Grace began to question whether or not her mother was even still alive. She lost twenty pounds that week because every time she went to eat, she saw her mother's face. It didn't help things that Michael blamed Grace for their mother's disappearance. Carrying all that guilt made it even more difficult for Grace to eat and even to want to live.

One evening, after a long day at work with no progress on the search for her mother and another unsuccessful attempt to eat, Grace sadly stepped out on to her little balcony.

Looking up towards the starry sky she cried out in desperation, "Who am I, but some dust on earth? What's been the use of struggling so hard for all these years? I am so very wounded and lonely having failed in marriage and now I might have even caused my mother to end her own life. What's the use of trying any longer?"

One Sunday, Grace called Pastor Scott and told him she was not going to church that day. She was depressed and didn't see the value of living anymore. She sat there alone, on the cold kitchen floor, leaning against one of the cabinets. Grace held out her arms and glanced at her wrists. Thoughts were flying through her mind. "This would end it all; all the pain, all the guilt, all the shame, all the failure, all the tough work...I won't have to face them anymore..."

Pastor Scott and his wife, Jenny were alert enough to skip service and go directly to Grace's apartment. It had been twenty minutes since Grace's phone call and they weren't far from Grace's apartment. They just prayed they'd be able to get to her in time.

Grace reached up to the counter above her head and grabbed a razor blade. She held it in her hand, staring at it. She had contemplated doing this before, but now she was actually going to.

"There was no other way," she told herself. "At least this way she wouldn't feel the guilt and heartache anymore. Life was just too hard and too cruel. Why should she have to endure it any longer? Hadn't she experienced enough pain already?"

"God wants me to be happy," she said arguing with herself. "If I do this I'll be free to be with Him...to be happy once again."

Grace closed her eyes, and just as she touched the blade to her wrist, she heard a knock at the door. She didn't want to talk to anyone. She didn't want anyone to see her like this. She ignored it. Looking back at the blade in her hands, she was about to apply pressure to her wrist when the knock came again, but this time it continued. The unceasing rapping on the door frustrated Grace and kept her from focusing on cutting herself. She sighed heavily with frustration as she angrily stood and marched towards the door.

As she opened the door, her eyes widened. Her pastors stood before her. The sun was bright, so Grace stayed within the darkness of the doorway. Pastor Scott took a long look at her, then took her by the arm and gently pulled her out into the sunlight. He could see that there were no lights on in the apartment, and all the blinds were closed. Grace obviously didn't want anyone to see her like this…especially them.

"Grace!" gasped Scott's wife, Jenny when she saw the emancipated girl in front of them. "You're so thin!"

She grasped the edge of Grace's dress which hung very loosely on her.

"Grace, what's happened to you?" asked Pastor Scott amazed she could have deteriorated so quickly.

Grace said nothing. She simply stood there gazing straight ahead. Jenny and Scott looked at each other for a moment, nodded to each other and then led Grace back inside. They sat her down in a chair and opened all the blinds. Jenny brought Grace a glass of water, then knelt down beside her.

"Grace, I know things have been stressful lately," she said as she tried to get Grace to make eye contact with her. "You have to tell us what's going on. We've never seen you like this before and we're very worried about you."

Grace remained silent, staring straight ahead.

"Please say something," Jenny pleaded.

"I think I know what's going on," Pastor Scott said, entering the room. "I found this on this kitchen floor."

He held up the blade Grace had intended to cut herself with. Jenny gasped as she stood and walked over to examine the blade. Pastor Scott handed the razor blade to her and she went back to Grace.

"Grace we understand that this is a very depressing situation for you, we really do. But this is not the answer," Jenny said holding the razor blade out in front of her.

Scott joined his wife at Grace's side and asked, "Why would you do this, Grace? Why?"

Suddenly, as though the floodgates had been opened, tears ran unchecked down Grace's face. Heart-wrenching sobs overtook her body as she placed her head in her hands.

She finally attempted to speak, "I'm just so miserable! I don't know where my mother is or if she's even alive. For all I know she's dead. And it's all my fault!"

"That's not true," Jenny said placing her hand on Grace's arm. "It's not your fault. You had nothing to do with this."

"I-I know," Grace sobbed, "but I can't help but feel guilty. If I hadn't have left, she may still be here and none of this would have ever happened!"

"I don't understand," said Pastor Scott. "You know God has been faithful to get you through every situation. You've seen His goodness in your own life time and time again. Why can't you trust Him just a little bit longer?"

"Grace," Jenny said as she hugged her tightly, "it's about time for you to forgive yourself! God already paid a hefty price for your mistakes; your sins, and your mom's, too. You have got to let go and let God take control!"

Those words stuck with Grace as she and the pastors talked the situation out. That night, the pastors called the elders of the church and had an intercessory prayer time for Grace. Grace began eating again, but only because her pastors and friends from church were keeping their eyes on her and making sure she ate and stayed healthy. Grace tried hard to keep her mind focused on work so that she would not constantly be thinking about her mother.

God is Faithful

Grace worked very hard and was glad to have something to keep her occupied during the day. Before Grace was hired at Universal Bank, she had actual gotten another job offer at a country club, but could not begin working there because they were still under construction. Months after taking the job at Universal Bank, Grace received an email from the man who had initially tried to hire her. He asked her to meet with him for lunch in order to discuss the job she had previously been offered. Politely, Grace refused the job telling him she was very happy at Universal Bank.

That night, Pastor Scott called Grace after their intercessory prayer time. He told Grace that God impressed on several members that Grace's mother was alive, and God will be dealing with her Himself. Out of the blue, Scott also mentioned to her that she should take the other job offer she had just received. To confirm whether it was God's will or not, Pastor Scott said they would offer her 10% more than what she was currently making without her telling them the exact amount of her present salary.

Grace was so depressed that she wasn't even sure she believed what he was saying. She simply thanked him and did not discuss it with him any further. Fifteen minutes later, her phone rang again. When she picked it up, she was shocked to hear her mother's voice.

"Mom?" Grace asked, shaking.

"I'm alive. I'm fine," were the only words Anne uttered before abruptly hanging up the phone.

Grace was relieved to learn that her mother was at least alive. Then she was stunned as she realized that Pastor's words had come true! Since the first part of what her pastor had spoken came to pass, she quickly made a decision about the call from the country club. Grace called to tell Pastor Scott about her mother's call and then told him she had decided to meet with Kevin about the job at the high-end luxury country club.

Grace met with Kevin, the man who had called her for the interview, at an American Business club where Kevin was the President. Grace felt a bit awkward as she walked in to see it filled with only businessmen. At the far end of the room, Grace spotted Kevin seated at a table by himself. After shaking Kevin's hand and seating herself in the empty chair across from him, they went through the business side of the job he was again offering her. She told him that she had come to talk with him for confirmation as to whether she was to take this job or not. Kevin was very excited to see her willingness to consider his offer.

"Is it about salary?" he asked.

"Yes," replied Grace.

"Well, that's simple," he said with a smile, "how much do you want? I am sure we can work things out."

"I-I can't tell you," Grace told him, knowing he was going to think her very strange.

"What?" he exclaimed loudly, obviously shocked by her response.

Everyone in the club looked over at them wondering what had happened to cause the sudden outburst.

"God told me He would tell you the exact amount," Grace said, deciding to lay it all on the table.

When Kevin heard this, Grace saw tears begin to form in his eyes. He told Grace that he had just become a believer a matter of weeks ago and felt his faith was being tested at this very moment!

Without looking at Grace, he took out his pen and prayed a quick prayer, "Lord, this isn't fair. You did not tell me a thing. I need You to tell me something—now."

They were both quiet for a bit. Then Kevin wrote down a number on the paper and slid it across the table to Grace.

"Is that the right figure?" he asked, obviously hoping she'd say it was.

Immediately, tears began to run down Grace's face. It was exactly 10% more than what she was making. She and Kevin quickly began discussing her employment. She couldn't wait to get home and call her church family!

Ask Yourself

- Do you believe in miracles? Have any miracles happened in your life? Share them with someone you care about.

- Have you ever felt as depressed as Grace did, with no desire to live? What changed your mind and convinced you life was worth living?

- Do you believe in the power of prayer, not just those "sound good" prayers, but prayers that carry power and manifestation? If your answer is yes, share your belief with someone you care about. If your answer is no, ask someone who knows about the power of prayer to help you to understand.

Chapter 8

What Is Forgiveness?

G race loved her church. After all she had been through with them, she knew these people truly cared about her. She wished she could go to church more than once a week. Though she went to her cell group on Tuesdays, she wished it could be every day. Though it was true her church family helped fill a part of the emptiness she felt inside, Grace was still very lonely since the divorce. She knew her marriage to Daniel had been unproductive, but she missed having him around. She missed having someone to come home to—someone to love.

She always looked for her "Mr. Right" everywhere she went. She knew she had to find a Christian man, but in her mind she just wanted to be with someone. Many nights she couldn't sleep. Her loneliness seemed to overtake her. In a conversation with Pastor Scott about this subject, he told Grace she needed to surrender it to God like she had her guilt over her mother and her need for the right job. She needed to follow whatever His plans were for her in every area of her life. Pastor assured her that God knew she did not want to be single for the rest of her life. He had given her that desire to marry. Despite this advice, Grace still found it difficult to give God full control.

One night, Grace had a terrible nightmare. She saw a huge black monster about to swallow her. Try as she might, she could not escape for it was pulling her in. She tried and tried to get away on her own, but could not. Terrified, Grace awoke in the middle of the night crying. She knew she must surrender everything to God if she wished to be free from the darkness.

Immediately, she got down on her knees and prayed, "Lord, I surrender. If You want me to be single from now on, fine. If You don't, fine. I know You love me enough, so I pray that Your will be done, not mine."

At that moment she felt a peace come over her—something she had not felt in many days.

Forgiveness Brings Forgiveness

It was Chinese New Year and Grace was alone at home. In her quiet time, she felt God nudged on her to forgive her ex-husband Daniel.

"Lord, I already forgave him, plus I know I made mistakes in that marriage, too," Grace wrote in her journal.

"Then give him a call to tell him that you have forgiven him," said a small voice ringing in her heart.

"God, you must be kidding me! How foolish I will look!" Grace complained.

The rest of the day Grace was restless and then someone gave her a verse: *"And when you stand praying, if you hold anything against anyone, forgive him, so that your Father in heaven may forgive you your sins."* (Mark 11:25).

"Lord, do I really have to?" Grace asked, still bargaining with God.

Finally, Grace picked up the phone and called Daniel on their former "home number."

"Hello, who is this?" a woman answered.

Grace almost hung up the phone right then, but she managed to compose herself enough to ask, "Hi, this is Daniel's old friend, may I know to whom I am speaking?"

"This is Daniel's wife, and you are Ms.?" the woman replied.

"I see, I just wanted to greet him and say Happy New Year, but since he is not around, that's okay," Grace said trying to get off the phone quickly as an emotional wave of shame, anger, and pain suddenly threatened to overwhelm her!

"Let me give you his cell phone number, I am sure he'd like to hear from an old friend," this new wife offered.

"Sure, that will be great!" Grace replied trying to keep her voice as "normal" as she could.

After she hung up with Daniel's "new wife," Grace stared at the piece of paper where she had written down his cell phone number.

"God, are you serious? He's married again already? That was fast and not at all fair! I am still here struggling with loneliness, and he already has a new wife!" Grace cried feeling angry and depressed all over again.

Then she was reminded of a recent conversation with a co-worker who told her, "If you have truly forgiven someone, then when you talk about what happened, you shouldn't feel too much emotion going on. In fact, being able to forgive empowers you to move on!"

At the thought of what her co-worker had shared, Grace felt a surge of resolve run through her spine and she knew she had to take action now.

"All right, Lord! I will give him a call right now, but You will have to be the one doing the talking, not me!" Grace said quickly, afraid she would lose her resolve.

Grace asked for God's "grace" to be able to make this phone call, then with trembling hands, she dialed Daniel's cell phone number.

"Hello?" Daniel's voice seemed so distant and unreal.

"Hi, Daniel, Happy New Year," Grace managed to say.

"Who is this?" Daniel asked.

Grace was thinking, "Gee, barely a year and already you cannot recognize my voice?!"

"It's Grace! How are you?" she said trying to remain calm.

There was a moment's silence before Daniel asked in a voice as cold as ice, "What do you want?"

"I just want to greet you, say Happy New Year, and congratulate you on your new marriage," Grace replied much more calmly then she was feeling.

"Okay, t-h-a-n-k you; but what exactly do you want from me?" Daniel asked suspecting there had to be more to this phone call.

"Well, this might sound odd, but I just want you to know I forgive you. I hope you will do the same for me and forgive me for the mistakes I made in our marriage," Grace said, finally managing to force the words she knew in her heart she needed to be said.

"Are you still single?" Daniel asked, catching Grace totally off guard.

She couldn't believe what she just heard, "Yes, I am; but what does that have to do with what I just said to you?"

"Well, I agree you made some serious mistakes in our marriage, so I'd suggest you don't be too picky as you look for a new mate. You *are* getting nearly too old to get married again," Daniel commented it in his usual authoritative voice.

Before Grace could respond, Daniel asked again, "Why did you call me? What do you *really* want from me?"

"As I said, I just want you to know I forgive you for what you did and to wish you a Happy New Year. That's all, nothing else! And I wish you and your new wife a very happy and long lasting marriage. Good-bye!" Grace managed to respond.

Grace held back her tears and swallowed her humiliation until she'd hung up the phone. Then she collapsed on the floor and cried until she had no tears left. Somehow the heavy weight she had carried these past few months left her. She felt much lighter as a sense of new beginning surrounded her.

Yet the temptation to try and find someone to fill that empty spot in her life did not stop. Grace joined the members of her church on a retreat where she met a man, who was single, charming, good looking, and a Christian. He and Grace spoke often over the course of the retreat and he seemed to be actively pursuing Grace. Thinking this was the case, Grace began asking God if this man was the one for her. On the third day of the retreat, Grace was both shocked and hurt to find out from a few of the other women there that this man she had been spending time with was to be married in a week. Grace knew she needed to keep her distance from him.

After returning from the retreat, Grace received several calls from Judas asking her out. Grace never answered the phone when he called but would still find several messages on her answering machine from him each evening. She fought against her own fleshly desires and asked God why this was happening.

"It isn't fair," she complained, "Lord, I am very lonely, and this is not the right man. Why does he keep calling and trying to tempt me?"

God used a teenager in her church to minister to Grace. They did not have a youth ministry because the church was very small, only about 200 people. Mary, who was only sixteen, was a very talented musician who often played guitar as she sang out prophecy. Mary loved Grace and treated her like her own sister. She called Grace one day out of the blue saying that God had something to tell her.

"This is going to sound strange," she said to Grace.

"Nothing coming from you is strange anymore," Grace chuckled.

"Do you have a pen and paper to write it down?" Mary asked then continued when Grace indicated she was ready.

"Well, God wanted me to tell you: 'You are My most precious woman. What you have done for Me, I see it all. You are My most precious bride. I love you dearly. I will reward you in abundance; just remember you are my precious bride!'"

"Does that make any sense to you?" Mary asked.

Grace was trembling as she wrote it down, then answered with a quiet, "Yes."

"Well good," Mary said, "God just wanted you to know that."

"Thank you!" Grace said sincerely as she hung up the phone.

She sat there stunned as she reread what she had written down. It was unfathomable to think that God would say that about her. She was so grateful for His love. It overwhelmed her.

The following Sunday when Pastor Scott asked her to contact Judas for some ministry ideas, Grace realized Judas was trying to get to her through Pastor Scott.

"That's not such a good idea," Grace told him.

"Why not?" Pastor Scott asked, obviously surprised by Grace's response to his request.

Grace explained to Pastor Scott what had been going on and then shared what God had said to her just a few days ago.

Another elder who had joined the conversation asked, "What more confirmation do you need?"

Grace thought about all that had happened in the last few weeks. As she recounted God's providence in every situation, including the call from her mother and giving her the job at the country club, she had to agree. She was still unsure as to why He had her take that job, and remain single but she knew He had a purpose.

Knowing she would be starting at the country club in a matter of days, Grace went in on Monday to officially resign from her job at Universal Bank. Her boss was puzzled when Grace told her she wasn't going to be working for another bank but was following God's will. Grace was getting used to people not understanding her reasoning, but she knew she was obeying God, and that's all that mattered to her right now. She was beginning to understand what it meant when her fellow Christians said they had learned to "walk by faith and not by sight."

Ask Yourself

- What does forgiveness mean to you?
- What would you do if you were Grace and God asked you to call Daniel?
- Why do you think Grace felt a lot "lighter" after she called Daniel? Who needed the phone call to happen more, Grace or Daniel?

Chapter 9

Walking by Faith Even at Work

G race was excited as she started her first day at The Club. She was surprised to find employees from many different nationalities working there. Grace was quickly introduced to the Vice President of Finance, Amy. Amy shared how happy she was to have Grace working for them.

"We interviewed so many people for this position, but we didn't feel right about hiring any of them until Kevin met you. He sent me the emails you had sent him asking very thorough questions about the job. I knew after reading them that we needed to hire you. When I relayed to Kevin that I wanted him to hire you, he shared with me about the salary story," Amy said with a chuckle.

"After your meeting with him that day, he came back truly touched. You see, I've known Kevin for about nine years now," Amy continued, "and I've been ministering to him ever since we first met. He just became a Christian a couple weeks before meeting with you. So after he told me about that experience with you, it was even more confirmation for me that we should hire you. I'd finally found someone who was as 'crazy for God' as I am extraordinarily happy to have you with us."

She hugged Grace, and then let her get back to her work. Grace was very blessed to hear the things Amy had said and realized once again

God was faithful to His promises. As she settled into her new job, she was also learning God was interested in every aspect of her life.

At the same time Grace's mother, Anne started calling her up again. Anne was still living with her boyfriend, Jo, which Grace found very difficult to understand. She knew their relationship wasn't healthy at all due to the drinking, fighting, and gambling. For Grace it seemed like such a big black hole her mother was in, though Anne couldn't see it or did not have the strength to pull herself out of it.

Grace also stayed connected with Michael who was still residing with his friend's family. She was thankful to God that he now had a wonderful job working for an European company, learning and growing at a very fast pace. Both Grace and Michael were aware their mother was still addicted to alcohol and gambling, though Grace often reflected, "But what can we do, she is our mom?" Grace wasn't giving up on her mom, she just realized only God could do what needed to be done in her mother's life. She continued to pray for both her mother and her brother as she learned to walk by faith in every area of her life.

Standing Firm by God's Promise

Grace's new job was proving to be very interesting. She was in charge of the membership Sales and Marketing Department. She was required to conduct intensive market research, map out marketing plans, and then execute those plans with her team for this multi-million dollar project, The Club. To say it was exciting and challenging was probably an understatement! She was also very aware that it was extremely rare for a woman of her age to be given a position of such importance.

About four months after Grace began working at the country club, a new executive in the Food & Beverage Department was hired named Christopher. He had relocated from Hong Kong though he was originally from Switzerland. To Grace's surprise, he spoke English very well. He didn't say much and most often kept to himself. He and Grace spoke occasionally, but Grace admired his quiet yet classy demeanor.

Other than Amy, everyone else who worked there were men and foreigners. There was an American Vice President, a Japanese Recreational Director, an Italian Chef, and now a Swiss Food & Beverage Director! With such a diversity of cultures, Grace often found she didn't get to speak her own language much and was constantly translating between Japanese and English for her colleagues. Pressure was heating up for all of them as the grand opening date got closer.

The Club itself was set to be at the finest level in the industry. The owner was from a very renowned social background and well connected in society. This was their first membership club investment, so they hired the top hotel designing firm for both the architecture and the interior design. They had invested millions to ensure The Club was the signature of the industry at the time, so there was very little room or tolerance for mistakes!

Grace and Amy looked into the general club market to determine what their enrollment fee should be. With so many clubs in the same district, they wondered how they were going to recruit enough members.

Most of the clubs charged a $6,000-7,000 (USD) enrollment fee and were having a hard time keeping enrollment up at that price. After much prayer and hours of intensive market research, Grace and Amy set the enrollment price at $8,000 (USD). Their budget required they enroll a minimum of 400 members before the grand opening, which was now only four months away.

Generally speaking, if enough people did not sign up for membership for a club like this within a set time period, that club would lower their enrollment fee. Everyone in the marketplace knew about this "strategy." However, Grace felt guided to raise the price if people did not respond within the first thirty days calling it a "Reverse-Marketing Strategy." It was risky, but after she researched and understood her target audience's behavior, Grace knew it would cause people to sign up as soon as possible knowing the price would go up, rather than waiting for the price to drop. Grace fully intended to make sure this was clearly communicated as they prepared for the grand opening festivities.

Grace had put her plan together, verified it with Amy and now she had to present her plan at a staff meeting. She was new and working to please a tough crowd. She couldn't afford any mistakes. There were plenty of people waiting for her to make that one fatal mistake. Jealously and female discrimination always permeated the atmosphere at these staff meetings. She already knew that, Ted, the General Manager, envied her great relationship with Amy and Kevin. He tried very hard to push her to her limit especially in front of her fellow employees.

After presenting her "Reverse-Marketing Strategy" and goals, Grace sat down and waited for the reactions of her peers. Ted was the first to respond to her presentation. He knew the goal of reaching four hundred members within four months was already setting the bar high, but Ted proposed raising it even higher.

"Why stop at 400 members?" he asked slyly, "Why not set the goal at 1000 so we will make the owner very happy?"

Grace felt her jaw drop but quickly gained control of herself knowing Ted was setting her up.

She remained calm and simply responded, "I need to go home and pray about it."

"Yeah, make sure your God can count!" Ted laughed, clearly mocking her.

With her mind screaming in protest and knowing what Ted was doing and why, she held herself in check, confident God led her here to work for purpose and would guide her in this as well. As Grace was praying that night asking God to reveal His plan whether they were to set their goal at 1,000 members or not, He showed her a verse in Psalm 44:3 that totally blew her mind. "It was not by their sword that they won the land, nor did their arm bring them victory; it was your right hand, your arm, and the light of your face, for you loved them." She read it and then read it again.

"Are you serious, Lord?" Grace asked realizing He was confirming she needed to set the goal at 1,000 members.

She had no idea how she was going to get that many members enrolled in such a short time, but as she continued to pray, God reassured her His grace was indeed sufficient! Reluctantly, Grace agreed and the next day she told Ted that they were going to go for 1,000 memberships instead of the 400 she had originally proposed.

He raised an eyebrow at her while issuing her a warning, "You do understand that when I write this down and submit it to the owner, it's no longer a possibility. It has to be achieved."

"I know," Grace said.

Ted shook his head and sighed as he wrote down the new goal. Grace knew he was thinking he needed to start looking for someone to replace her because he certainly did not believe she could get all those memberships in time. There was a part of Grace that didn't believe she could do it either, but it was too late to go back. She had believed this was God's plan so it was in His hands now.

God is Faithful Even in the Storm

After weeks of planning and researching, Amy guided The Club to purchase top-of-the line stationary and print 9,000 well-designed announcements that invited local companies, businesses owners and their employees to attend The Club's grand opening and take advantage of a thirty-day introductory membership registration offer. Grace and the other executives worked late into the night to hand-fold the letters, and carefully slide them into the envelopes to be mailed the following day.

It seemed though that nobody really believed The Club would actually raise their prices if people did not sign up within the first thirty days.

Grace knew her resolve would be tested but she didn't expect it to happen through a literal storm! About a week later a typhoon hit Tai Pei. It was not an unusual occurrence for the area as Taiwan is located on a tropical island, but it discouraged Grace. Potential members would be even more disinclined to sign up, not wanting to leave their homes in the middle of a typhoon. Though no one had to go in to work the day the typhoon hit, Grace went in anyway. Since she knew nobody else would be there she wore shorts and a tank top. As she stood at her desk looking for some papers, she did not notice Kevin come up behind her.

When she turned around, she let out a scream, "W-what are you doing here?"

"Me?" he asked, "What are you doing here?"

"Well, I'll tell you what I'm not doing," she blurted out, "I'm not sneaking up behind people and scaring them half to death!"

Kevin grinned and let out a hearty laugh.

"It's not funny!" Grace exclaimed as she slapped him on the arm and tried not to laugh, "No one was supposed to be here."

"So why are you here?" Kevin asked.

"I just figured I'd get some work done, get organized since I have nothing else to do," she responded, "What about you?"

"The same. Just getting organized before another busy day hits," he explained. "Either I work today or I work on Saturday, which my wife wouldn't be too happy about."

"I see," Grace said, "then I guess I'll let you get back to work."

"By the way, since you are local could you do me a favor and invite the Swiss guy and the Japanese guy to a movie and dinner so you guys can build up a friendlier inter-work relationship between you?" Kevin asked with a grin.

"Sure, boss," Grace answered thinking what such an evening would look like; the Swiss guys couldn't understand Japanese, and the Japanese guy knew very little English.

"It will certainly make for a very interesting dinner!" she added, not necessarily looking forward to this assignment.

Grace and Kevin returned to their work while Grace kept an eye out for any more surprise visitors. Several minutes later, Grace heard a knock on the door which she had carefully locked thinking she was going to be working alone in the office.

"Who could that be? Why would anyone come here during a typhoon?" she thought.

As she approached the entrance, she saw a young couple smiling at her through the glass. They quickly informed Grace that they had received the invitation letter and were interested in a possible membership.

"We thought since we don't have to work today," they explained, "we would stop by and find out about the offer The Club had for early membership registration."

"Sure, come in," she invited, thankful she was not alone in the building.

Suddenly embarrassed by her informal attire, she quickly added, "Please excuse my dress code today. I wasn't expecting any clients on this typhoon day."

The couple burst into laughter, as they pointed out they were also wearing shorts and t-shirts. Grace chatted comfortably with them as she ushered them into a conference room. She discovered that they were Christians, which she thought was very interesting since less than 2% of the population were Christians at the time. At the end of the meeting, this young Christian couple became her first enrolled members!

Grace felt such an overwhelming love for God who had sent a Christian couple to assure her that He is with her and would fulfill His plans for her, even during a stormy typhoon!

Ask Yourself

- Have you done something at the workplace that required you to walk by faith? If yes, share it with someone you care about.

- How do you generally make business decisions? Do you believe there is a "higher" wisdom to tap into instead of relying solely your own experience and expertise?

- If you were Grace, would you have had the courage to take up the challenge set by Ted?

Chapter 10

Achieving the Impossible

A nother week had flown by. Grace and her team were picking up momentum in enrolling members; it was obvious that God was at work! Even though things were extremely busy at The Club, Grace invited the Food & Beverage Director and the Recreation Director for a movie and dinner since Kevin had asked her to show some them local hospitality.

"Where's Akio?" Grace asked when only Christopher, the new Food & Beverage Director showed up to meet her in front of the cinema on Saturday evening.

"He's still tied up in a meeting with his crew," Christopher answered with a smile.

Not sure how she should feel about this, Grace was left with only Christopher for the evening. After the movie, they went to have coffee. Grace could not believe how much Christopher spoke that night. He was always so quiet and mild-mannered at work. Grace enjoyed his company very much and began to feel an attraction toward him. He was good looking, charming, funny, polite; possessing all the characteristics Grace loved in a friend. But was he the one God had for her to become more than just a friend? After they said good-night, she decided to invite him to attend a church service with her in the near future and go from there.

Miracles

There was little time to think of dating as The Club kicked up the momentum! Within a month, Grace and her sales team had enrolled over 400 members at the introductory membership discount. As the first month of business came to an end, they kept their word and raised the price of membership from $8,000 to $10,000 (USD). The people who had signed up early were very glad that their membership already increased in value!

But those who had not yet signed up were upset that the prices had risen and continually asked for discounts. Almost daily, Grace had to refuse many prospects, but stayed true to her "Reverse-Marketing" strategy. However, they did decide to mail out letters again to notify potential members that there were only two weeks left to sign up before prices went up again. This time people realized The Club was really going to do it and poured in like crazy! Grace had to hire more sales managers to handle the increased volume.

While all this craziness was going on, Grace's mother suddenly appeared and asked Grace for money. Grace did not want to abandon her mother, so she gave her a decent amount of money, but made Anne promise not to use it on gambling or alcohol, otherwise she would not receive any more help from Grace. Anne promised, but Grace knew she would soon have gambled it all away again. She sent a quick prayer up to God for her mother knowing He was the only One that could really help. She had already seen so many miracles, even in her brother Michael's life. Michael had landed himself a high-paid sales job and had a bright career ahead of him. He visited Grace from time to time to catch up.

Since their accidental "date," Christopher had asked Grace out for a couple more dinner dates. Grace was excited but reserved and decided to follow through on her idea to invite him to attend her church cell group on Tuesday instead of going to dinner. She explained that Pastor Scott and her friends were her only real family now and felt it was important for Christopher to get to know them. He was unable to attend on Tuesday but agreed to go with her to church on Sunday. After service, Pastor Scott approached them and after they talked for a bit, he invited Christopher to have breakfast with him the next day.

"Oh boy," Grace thought, getting through to him would be difficult but she knew the issue of Christopher's faith was standing in the way of their relationship progressing any further. If anyone could reach Chris, it was Pastor Scott. For her, faith in the one true God was the only way to establish the solid foundation they would need if they were to have a future life and family together. "Now," she thought, "I might find out if he was the one."

Grace didn't find out until later all that transpired at this breakfast meeting between Pastor Scott and Christopher.

The Christopher Miracle

The next morning at breakfast with Pastor Scott, Chris shared his belief in all the different religions, energy, etc. He admitted he did not necessarily understand everything they did at their church and expressed concerned surprise at how much of her income Grace gave to the church and different causes. He knew her income was more than his so she was giving away a lot of money! Chris willingly shared that he enjoyed being able to believe in whatever he thought made the most sense for whatever circumstance he was facing at the time. He shared that he had left home very early to stand on his own feet and he didn't see the need to put his faith in a "Heavenly Father."

Pastor Scott listened patiently and then asked, "What was your church experience in Switzerland?"

"Well, it was more like you showed up for attendance, then sat through a boring and useless service. We basically only go to church for few occasions like weddings, Christmas, and funerals. We don't have the 'Spirit-led' thing you guys mentioned on Sunday," Chris replied.

"I got to say," he admitted, "although I am not able to get my head around it, I can't deny what I see happening in Grace's life. She has so many stories of how she has followed God and come through one event after another; that's pretty impressive."

Out of a fatherly love for Grace, Pastor Scott approached her later and expressed his concern about their relationship based on what God says about being unequally yoked to an unbeliever.

"We cannot change people, you know that, don't you?" Pastor Scott said to Grace.

"Yes, I know," Grace sadly agreed, "I can only pray and leave it to God."

Grace invited Chris to come along to the weekly small group gathering where the hosts were Swiss, too. This lovely couple, John and Mary, were thrilled to meet their fellow country man. Chris found the group of men, who were from different generations (grandpas, fathers, sons), very inspiring as they supported each other and freely shared with each other the challenges they were each facing and the joy they were experiencing in their individual lives.

Chris continued attending the small group and church services. To Grace's pleasant surprise, one Saturday evening he shared with her how deeply touched he had been by them all. The following Sunday, as they stepped into church shortly before the service started, Chris left Grace alone without saying a word and walked up to Pastor Scott.

Wondering what was going on? Grace prayed. Chris came back to the seat next her with a smile on his face, still saying nothing about his conversation with Pastor Scott. The service started with Pastor

Scott announcing the date for the next baptismal service. When he asked those who were ready to be baptized to raise their hands, Chris raised his! Grace was speechless to say the least!

"What on the earth, Chris?" Grace was barely able to ask.

"You should be saying *Congratulations*, instead of asking me a question, right?" Chris teased her.

"Yes, of course, congratulations...but what happened?" Grace asked still trying to comprehend what just happened.

"Tell you later," Chris said with a big grin.

After the service, they went to greet Pastor Scott who was wearing a big smile as he asked, "Did Chris tell you the vision?"

"What vision?" Grace asked, even more in the fog.

"The vision God showed him," Pastor Scott explained, "the one that prompted him to make the decision to get baptized."

Chris was just standing there smiling and obviously enjoying each minute of it.

"I guess we have quite a lot to talk about, don't we, Chris!" Grace said as she tried to wrap her head around the whole thing.

As they finally sat down for lunch in their favorite restaurant, "So?" Grace asked, hardly able to contain herself.

"Well, the other night at the small group meeting when we broke up into the separate men and women's circles to pray for each other, one brother prayed over me, then I started seeing things..."

"What things?" Grace asked excitedly.

"Well, I had decided I needed to find out if God really existed so I asked Him that if He truly existed, to show me Himself strong. During the prayer, I started seeing a cross with a ring, then many stars in the sky around my heart."

"Which means Commitment!" they both burst out at the same time.

"So I know He is real and that all the stories you guys have told me and all that has happened in front of my eyes in last few months, it's all real!" Chris shared with a voice filled with emotion, "I feel so much joy inside of me, and I know it's time for me to commit to God!"

Tears rose up in Grace's eyes, God answered her prayer again **big time**! There were no words to describe how overwhelmed she was to hear what Chris just said.

"Thank you, Lord!" she exclaimed as they gave each other a big hug.

The Club Miracles

In the meantime, The Club continued to gain more and more members as the months rolled by. Near the end of the third month, The Club had reached 900 members. Grace grew nervous as they only had one more week to get 100 more members left to enroll. Grace prayed continually and never stopped believing God would come through. This was His will. He would make it happen. Midway through the week, they had seventy-five more members.

As Grace was about to leave on Wednesday evening, Ted approached her, "Only two more days and you're still twenty-five members short."

"We've had seventy-five sign-ups in the past seventy-two hours," Grace reminded him, "I don't think getting twenty-five more will be a problem."

"Are you sure? Twenty-five memberships is a lot to expect in only two days. You know how business is constantly fluctuating from fast to slow to fast again," he taunted. "But since you don't seem to be worried I suppose I should wish you luck."

"I have God's blessing, that's all I need. You can keep your luck," she told him as she brushed passed him and headed out the door. "Have a great evening."

By the week's end, God had fulfilled His promise and brought in 1000 memberships. Everyone celebrated the miracle that had occurred. Grace continued to be astonished at God's goodness and faithfulness. The Club's grand opening was spectacular, as they broke many other records in the industry!

Time to Change

After achieving 1000 members and a successful grand opening, a new American general manager named Randy was hired at The Club. Randy quickly became quite jealous of Grace's influential position and relationship with the staff. As promised by the upper management team, after the grand opening Grace received the green light to allow her team to each take turns having one month's vacation to compensate the day-offs they didn't get to have in the pre-opening stage. By this time, many of them had already scheduled vacations with their families and booked flights.

One afternoon, one of Grace's sales managers came to her crying, saying Randy had refused to let any of them take their scheduled vacations. Confused, and a bit outraged, Grace went in to speak with Randy. To her surprise, he still refused.

"They have worked very hard and we've already promised them that they can have these vacations," Grace explained. "We as a company made the promise to staff members, we must honor our words!"

"Well, It happened before my arrival, I'm the boss now, and you need to obey me," Randy warned, "otherwise you're fired."

"Yes, I understand that you're the boss," Grace responded, attempting to keep her composure, "But why can't you let them take the vacations they've been promised?"

Randy refused to give Grace any reasonable explanation for his decision and ended any further discussion on the subject by saying, "Either you're going to tell them, or I will."

"I'm sorry, I have to stick to [our] words," she said as she stood to leave, "Let's discuss this with Kevin later."

As she walked towards the door, Grace was stopped by Randy's next words, "If you walk out that door, you're fired."

"If that's the way it has to be, so be it!" she declared as she opened the door and exited the office to find all of her sales managers eagerly waiting to hear the results of her meeting.

"I'm sorry," she said, shaking her head sadly, "I tried, I really did. But I'm afraid I couldn't get him to agree to your vacations and I can't come back to work here anymore."

She saw the devastation on their faces as they realized what she was saying. She hugged them all good-bye and walked sadly but regally out the door. Later that night, she called both Kevin and Amy and explained what had happened. Unfortunately, Amy had no control over the situation, and Kevin insisted that he needed to keep Randy on staff.

"If you feel you need to keep him, then do what you need to do," Grace told Kevin, "but I won't be coming back."

The next day Grace sent in her letter of resignation. Three months later, Grace heard from Amy that Randy had been fired due to some silly mistakes he made. Upon hearing about the situation with Randy and some other changes that were occurring at The Club, Christopher decided he would resign as well. As they both had semi-high profile resumes, Grace and Christopher were confident they'd easily find new jobs. However, after a few weeks of searching and mailing over twenty resumes to companies in Taiwan and other Asian countries, they still had not had even one interview between them. They couldn't help wondering what God was up to.

Meanwhile, Grace and Christopher's relationship continued to grow stronger and they started talking about their future. One evening after dinner, Christopher told Grace he had something to ask her.

"What is it?" asked Grace curiously.

Christopher pulled a small, velvet box out of his pocket. As he got down on one knee, he opened it, revealing a beautiful gold ring.

Grace gasped.

"Will you marry me?" he asked her.

Grace was speechless. She simply stood staring at him with her hands over her mouth.

"Please say something," he urged after several moments, still down on one knee in front of her.

Grace had prayed to God many times asking Him if this was the man for her. She felt in her heart that God had said yes, but she didn't want to make the wrong decision again. She silently prayed once more asking God what she should do. After a moment, she felt a peace in her heart to say yes. Overjoyed she felt tears begin to run down her face.

"Yes!" she exclaimed as Christopher stood to his feet and she embraced him tightly.

The ceremony at their church was beautiful, and Grace was filled with overwhelming happiness and joy in knowing she would forever be with someone she loved and that God had prepared for her.

As they continued looking for jobs after their wedding with no viable offers, "It is all really strange," Grace thought. She had seen so many miracles already in her life, she diligently prayed for God's direction knowing He had a plan for them. One night as Grace was praying about it, she felt God telling her that they needed to move back to Switzerland where Chris grew up. Grace did not like the thought of leaving her home in Asia. Not only was Switzerland a different country, it was on a whole different continent. The idea of moving away from her own country with total different languages, cultures, and lifestyle almost freaked Grace out.

However, God surely had His hands on Chris as well. Grace discovered God had spoken the same thing to Chris so they realized that this was a necessary move. They had no clue why, but they had learned to tune in with God's voice and obey His directions. They wasted no time in packing up and preparing to move. Grace was four months pregnant at this time and lifting heavy boxes was too strenuous. She figured she would stick to organizing and labeling the boxes and let Chris do the lifting. Within two weeks, they had packed all their belongings and were ready to head to Switzerland.

Grace was still not fond of the idea of leaving the only home she'd ever known. Asia was so dear to her and the thought of living so far away from it filled Grace with great anxiety. She had no idea what to expect but was thankful they would be staying with Chris's parents, so at least there would be some familiarity. Grace liked her husband's parents very much and was grateful that they had opened their home to them during this transactional time. They had all worked and lived abroad so they all spoke English. Grace thanked God often for Chris' family as she prepared to leave the familiar and move into the unknown.

Ask Yourself

- How important is it to you to be able to keep your word? At what price?

- Why do you think Grace was waiting on Chris' decision to be baptized?

- What does "believing in God" mean to you? Does it require any action on your part? Explain.

Chapter 11

Living Abroad, the Humbling Process Has Begun

L eaving the airport after landing in Switzerland, Grace was already feeling homesick. As they drove to Chris' parents' house, Grace observed how small the cities in Switzerland were compared to the city of over seven million people where she had grown up. Everything seemed smaller and was so very different. The buildings, the layout of the town—nothing here was what she was used to. In Asia, the stores were pretty much open twenty-four hours a day, seven days a week so there were always people coming and going on the street. In Switzerland, the stores were generally only open until 4:00 p.m. and closed on Sundays. It was too quiet for Grace sometimes.

The Humbling Process Begins

Two months after they had settled into Chris' parents' home, Grace sensed that for some reason she was always "watched."

She couldn't really prove it until one day after she had gone to Zurich to run some errands, Chris' Mom asked, "Did you have good time?"

"Yes, I did, Mom. I liked the English bookstore very much," Grace replied.

"I knew you would. Mrs. Zuller said she thought you enjoyed your time there," Mom said.

"Who is Mrs. Zuller?" Grace asked trying to place the name, "I don't remember meeting anyone I knew at the bookstore."

"Oh, I don't think you met her yet, but she had seen your photo and she happened to be in the bookstore today as well," Mom patiently explained. "She just called me to let me know she thought she had seen you there."

"I see," Grace replied, feeling a little stunned at first by this information.

However, she knew there were hardly any Asians living in the city and her parents-in-law were well connected in the local society, so Grace realized she could be spotted very easily.

One of the first things they had to do once they got settled in was to open a bank account.

As Grace and Chris sat in front of the account supervisor at the bank, the language barrier made it difficult for Grace to understand the questions the supervisor was asking Chris.

"What did they say, honey?" Grace asked when the woman went to get some paperwork.

Chris appeared hesitant to tell her but said, "Well, they are asking how much access I want to allow you to the account."

"What?" Grace said, shocked and hurt by this, "Did you tell them that more than 70% of the money is from me?"

Grace had gone from being super independent in her career, to where she had no choice but to entrust everything to her husband, the only name on the account. Grace was not a citizen and she couldn't even apply for a Swiss passport until she had been married for six years. The humbling process caused by living in a totally different culture had only just begun.

Realizing language was going to be a problem for her even though her in-laws spoke English, Grace enrolled in a German school to learn the language. Although the Swiss people could speak German, and all their official documents were written in German, they spoke a distinctly unique Swiss-German dialogue in their daily conversations. These two languages were so different that Grace had a hard time learning much of it at all. After taking the class in German, Grace still could not communicate with her neighbors or store clerks.

Though Grace liked the serene environment Switzerland provided, she felt imprisoned there. She was used to being an independent business woman, but now she was dependent on everyone around her and had to adjust to life as a house wife and soon-to-be mom. They lived out of two suitcases and had fifty-two boxes in storage. Grace hated all this change and felt helpless for the first several months. Out of love, her mother-in-law wanted to pay for everything which made Grace feel even more incapable of providing for herself. She was used to having control of the way she lived and liked being able to support herself. Why couldn't things just go back to how they used to be?

A Beautiful Snowy Foreign Land

It was mid October when the snow started falling in Switzerland. Snow was new to Grace. She had never experienced a snowy day in her life. She remembered when she was little, watching an American movie related to Christmas and thinking how nice it would be to one day enjoy a snowy white Christmas with her loved ones in their own home. In Asia most people even could not afford to have their own home, the cost of real estate was so high.

"Odd," she thought, "I feel so lonely in this beautiful snowy foreign land." Then she realized it was because she missed her homeland; she missed Chinese food, she missed her friends and she missed her church. Grace and Chris had visited a few churches, but so far there was not one in the neighborhood which they felt they fit in with.

One thing was sure, Grace was never really alone. Almost daily she felt the movement of the baby a lot. After numerous ultrasound visits they still couldn't figure out whether it was a girl or a boy, as the baby was in the "bridge-sitting" position. Grace and Chris were praying and asking God for the baby's name, since they had no idea whether it would be a girl or a boy. At the same time, they hoped the baby could turn to the right position in time or Grace would have to go through a C-section to give birth. The thought of having to have surgery in a foreign environment terrified her!

She could not understand phone calls, television programs, or newspapers. Most days she would come home crying because of the frustration she felt from not being able to communicate with anyone outside her family. As Chris' family was highly regarded and well connected in the community, there were often guests there for meals or coffee. Grace only could smile for hours, unable to understand a word of what the conversation was about. The self-esteem of being able to master two foreign languages in Asia and successfully attaining a high achieving career seemed totally useless to her now. Shame, insecurity, frustrations, and mood swings came upon her like a big wave and threw her totally out of control! "Lord, what are You doing to me?" Grace often wondered.

Four months after they relocated to Switzerland, Christopher found a job. While he worked, Grace was left at home to take care of the house and do the shopping. The grocery store was within walking distance and it did not take Grace very long to get there. Grace did not understand any Swiss/German, so communicating with the people at the store was useless. Grace was able to find the things she needed, but the store only took cash, so when the cashier would try to tell Grace how much she owed, she could not understand. She felt so lost and frustrated.

Suddenly Christmas was upon them. It was Grace's very first Christmas away from Taiwan. Although in Taiwan Christmas wasn't widely celebrated, Grace had always loved getting together with her church family and decorating the tree together. Grace loved to gaze upon all the twinkling lights and beautiful ornaments. Then they would sing songs, recite the true meaning of Christmas and Pastor Scott's wife, Jenny would bake a lot of cookies to spoil them after the service.

How she missed Asia and her friends. As Grace reminisced about Christmases past, she realized it snowed in Switzerland for most of the winter. She gazed out her window and saw nothing but snow-capped mountains and a crystal white landscape. It hadn't stopped snowing for days. Grace felt a jolt of happiness surge through her as she realized that she had finally gotten her white Christmas! She thanked God for granting her wish this year so that she could once again feel the joy and wonder of the Christmas season.

"Oh, Lord! Thank you, for this beautiful snowy foreign land. I am sorry that I didn't recognize it earlier."

Motherhood

It was January, ten day past the baby's due date when Grace's water broke finally. As they rushed her to the hospital, Grace felt panic and terror overtook her. She still hadn't adjusted to living in a foreign land and now she would have to learn to be a mother, which she didn't know anything about either.

As labor increased and the contractions started coming more frequently, the doctor examined Grace and baby.

"This is not good," the doctor explained to the family in German, "the baby is still in bridge position so we need to perform a C-Session. The baby is too large for us to try to deliver by natural birth."

As the doctor continued to explain, Chris tried to translate as quickly as he could for Grace. Within thirty minutes Grace was placed on the operating table, but due to the language barrier, she couldn't understand a word the medical team was saying. She felt like a piece of meat being flipped around as they gave her all sorts of injections and prepared her body for surgery. In her head, she told herself everything they were doing was to help her and the baby. However, in her heart, she felt terribly alone and scared as streams of tears ran down her cheeks, she prayed "God help me," over and over as she awaited the birth of her child.

After experiencing tremendous pressure from her chest down, the doctor delivered her baby.

"It's a girl!" the nurse announced in English to Grace, "and she is a very big girl! 4.2 kilograms!" the nurse announced as the whole operating room was filled with joy and amazement at how such a tiny Asian lady could have such a jumbo baby! Baby Emily had finally arrived!

Grace was overcome with a feeling of such love and joy as the nurse placed her baby girl in her arms. But that joy was short lived as Grace soon became severely depressed. For some reason she couldn't control her emotions. She found herself easily slipping in and out a sadness that left her with no interest for anything. The time of recovery from the C-Section was tough on her. She wasn't able to walk much for the first week and instructed to take as much rest as she could. The nurses taught both parents everything they needed to know about how to take care of their baby. They were all very friendly but none of them spoke much English.

Every day they would bring her a menu that she could not read. Chris was at work during the day so he could not translate it for her. The hospital food was very different from that in Asia. Asians believed very strongly in healthy eating, especially after giving birth or undergoing surgery. It was traditional to feed patients warm nutritional soups to help them recover. In Switzerland, however, though they too emphasized healthy eating, they served things such as cold yogurt to help patients recover. Every day when meal time came, Grace would cry because she was not used to eating the food. She found herself feeling very stressed more often than not.

"Lord, this is very difficult for me, I am like a blind and deaf person," she cried, "I don't understand what people around me are saying and they cannot understand me, either. I need help, God! The responsibility of being a new mother in a foreign land is making me crazy."

One day the medical team gave Grace a document about breast feeding. Grace tried to explain that she could not understand it. They assigned her a nurse who spoke very little English. Grace struggled to try and communicate with her but it was no use. The nurse could barely say "hello" and "good-bye" in English. She could not help Grace at all.

After three days of frustration, a new nurse entered her room and greeted Grace in Chinese. Grace was so astonished, she found herself replying to the nurse in English.

"Oh, I thought you spoke Chinese," the nurse said in English.

"Yes, I do speak Chinese as well," Grace replied, relieved to finally have someone she could clearly communicate with.

God had once again heard her heart cry! That night, Grace and the nurse spoke for a very long time. Grace discovered that this woman was half German and half Chinese. She lived on the border between Germany and Switzerland. When Grace explained how she could not understand the document she had been given in German, the nurse went home and translated the entire document into Chinese. Grace was truly grateful to have her there for the remainder of her stay at the hospital.

After several days, Grace was released from the hospital and sent home. Still recovering from surgery, she was unable to do much. She came home to a pile of laundry which she would have to drag down to the first floor of the apartment complex to wash. She knew she needed to get all that laundry done, as well as iron Chris's work shirts, but she was not permitted to lift anything heavier than a water glass.

As she stood there trying to figure out what to do, there came a knock at the front door. She opened the door to find a woman standing there who looked to be several years older than Grace.

The woman introduced herself in English before even being invited in. As Grace shook her hand and led her into the apartment, the woman relayed that she was a friend of the Swiss couple in Grace's cell group back in Taiwan. Grace could not believe it! Grace also learned that she was one of the top salespeople in selling ironing machines. She glanced at the bedroom with a pile of dirty dressed shirts laundry.

"I can help you with that laundry," she offered.

"Thank you, but I'm fine," Grace smiled politely.

"Alright, I'll come by tomorrow at nine and we can chat for a bit," said the woman as she headed for the door.

She didn't even wait for Grace to let her out as she opened the door and exited the apartment. Grace observed that she was a bit of a forceful woman and definitely independent. The next day she showed up right on time. She and Grace wasted no time in getting to know each other. After conversing for a few hours, the woman glanced once again at the pile of laundry in the bedroom.

"When are you going to do that?" she asked pointing to the dirty clothes.

"Soon," Grace replied as she stirred her tea.

"Tell you what," her neighbor offered, "I'll take it with me, wash it, and then bring it back to you by tomorrow morning. How's that sound?"

"Well, thank you," Grace replied, "but that's really not necessary."

"No more 'buts'," the woman protested as she walked into the living room and began gathering up the clothes, "I'll have these back to you before you can blink."

With that, she was off. She returned the next day just as she had promised with the clothes all clean and pressed. Grace could not thank her enough. Grace wished that Pastor Scott and family were there with her so she could share with them all the things God had done to bless her during this rough time. She missed her old church dearly.

She and Christopher had been searching for a church in Switzerland for some time now and had finally found one in Zurich they liked very much. It was similar to her old church and held cell groups once a week. Grace and Chris offered to have their group meet at their home on Tuesday nights. The group consisted of ten people, each from a different nation.

God, Please Help My Mother

Just as Grace began to feel more settled in Switzerland, her mom, Anne started calling her and asking for financial support. After communicating with her brother, Michael, Grace knew Anne was still involved in gambling and drinking. Grace's heart was torn between cultural expectations and her own core values. The Chinese culture expects her to always say "Yes" to parents regardless of the circumstances, but Grace knew if she continued to give Anne money, it would not help.

Anne was often drunk and crying when she called. Grace would weep after she hung up the phone with Anne!

"Grace, hey little girl, how are you?" came Anne's voice as she called late one night.

"Mom, I am fine, are you drinking again?" Grace demanded.

"No, no, no," Anne replied in her noisy drunken voice, "I was just thinking when we were all together for Chinese New Year, we'd play games and you'd always lose. Do you remember that?"

"Mom, it's expensive for overseas calls, why not you go rest and when you are in clear mind, then we can talk," Grace said not wanting to relive those painful memories and trying to shorten this unproductive conversation.

"I really need some more money, so I can buy some food and clothes," Anne suddenly pleaded.

"Mom, didn't Michael and I just give you $3,000 a little while ago?" Grace asked, "You need to find a job to support yourself and stop gambling or drinking it away. Just listen to yourself now, you sound half drunk already!"

"Wow, listen to that! How dare you are to speak to your own mother like that?" Anne cried, "Remember how hard I worked to raise you up! Did you forget it all already?"

All the shame, guilt, and heartache rose up in her mind as Grace remembered how Anne had mocked her and her pastor the day she moved out. Unpleasant memories of life with Anne and her boyfriend all flood Grace's mind as she listened to her mother's drunken voice.

"Mom, I'm sorry. I have to hang up now, it's really late," Grace said as she hung up and wept!

Even this far away, Grace still felt she was living under the darkness of the old days whenever Anne called.

"Father God, I feel so helpless!" Grace prayed, "I am so far away from her, I cannot do more, and I don't know how to help her to realize what kind of darkness she is living in!"

As Grace was collapsed on the floor weeping, she heard the inner voice from the Lord, "Grace, this is part of the reason why I needed to move you out of Taiwan. If you are there, you are her god. You would always supply what she needs, then she would never wake up and come to find Me."

"Lord, please help my mother, help her to wake up and find You," Grace pleaded.

Ask Yourself

- What kind of process was Grace going through after they moved to Switzerland?

- What was the impact of this move on Grace and Chris' marriage?

- Express your thoughts and feelings in the scene when Anne called Grace for money in Switzerland. Would you have done things differently?

Chapter 12

It's a Piece of Cake for God

G race loved being involved in church again, but as time passed she grew to miss her old church and home even more. At the same time, Chris also missed the "fast-paced" working style in the luxury hotel chains he was used to in Asia. When their daughter Emily was two years old they decided to take the Asia trip to visit friends and family, and also to distribute Chris' resumés to hotels there.

They were so glad to be able to meet up with many old colleagues, friends, Grace's mom and brother. Two weeks flew by so quickly and it was hard to say good-bye again. Grace was able to catch up with her pastors and introduce Emily to everyone before they returned to Switzerland.

Shortly after returning from their Asia trip, Chris received a letter from one of the hotels he sent his resumé to. Only it wasn't from a hotel in Singapore, but in Jamaica. The manager invited Chris to travel to Jamaica for an interview with them. Chris and Grace rejoiced over the good news, but really had no clue what Jamaica had to offer. Grace immediately began doing extensive research on Jamaica and after discovering that the crime rate was high and poverty was off the charts, she made up her mind that she did not want to go. She was firm on her decision and was resolved to stay in Switzerland, but after some heavy negotiating on Chris's part, she reluctantly agreed to go to the interview with him.

They left Emily with her Grandparents and took an early morning flight to Jamaica. The resort area was very nice, but everywhere else in Jamaica was very dirty and poverty-stricken. The job interview couldn't have gone better and the hotel wanted Chris to sign the contract with them right then, but Grace was unsure. They toured many properties they might possibly rent for their family, but the rental on each was at least $2,000 (USD), way over their budget, and many of them were just too filthy. That night, Grace and Chris had been invited to dinner at the hotel with the general manager and his wife. The manager tried everything he could to sell Chris on the job. Chris was very interested and really wanted to sign with them, but he knew it was just as much Grace's decision as it was his.

"How was your tour today, Chris? Wasn't the beach beautiful?" the general manager asked.

"Absolutely gorgeous!" Chris replied.

"Wouldn't it be nice to work with this kind of scenery every single day?" the manager persisted.

"Well, my wife would need to agree with it, we are family here," Chris looked at Grace, as did the general manager and his wife.

"What do you think?" the general manager asked Grace.

Grace thought, "Great! Now I have to be the bad guy."

"Well," she began, "I must say I'm not too pleased with the residential areas that we've seen so far. None of them are in our budget and almost all of them are dirty and poorly kept. I am not so sure yet whether this will be the right move for us and our family."

A Fountain in the Midst of Darkness

They took a week to continue looking at properties. On Sunday they went to a local church, they were the only foreigners there. Because poverty ruled most of the land, the church was constructed of four poles and a sheet on top to form a tent with chairs so that people could sit. It was extremely hot outside, yet it was like an old English movie Grace had seen where the women wore lace dresses and hats and the men wore suits. The Pastor also wore a white suit. You could tell they put on their best for Sundays.

The service started with worship and continued for a long time. After an hour, Grace and Chris began to wonder when the preaching would start. Two hours into worship, the pastor began to lay hands on people. Grace watched as one-by-one, each person he laid hands on fell to the ground in the Spirit. He slowly made his way back to Grace and her husband.

"Lord, please don't let him touch me," Grace prayed softly.

"Are you two married?" the pastor asked them.

"Yes," Chris quietly responded.

"God has something to tell you," the pastor said as he began to pray over them.

He barely touched them and they both went down. Grace saw complete darkness, but in the middle of it was a fountain which lit up. After getting up, Grace asked Chris what he had seen. He described something similar to what Grace had seen and they both knew God was telling them they needed to move to Jamaica and go to that church.

On the way home to Switzerland, Grace reluctantly agreed to let Chris return alone to Jamaica and if he could find a decent house for them, then Grace and Emily could relocate and he could sign the contract. Grace was confident that Chris would not be able to find a suitable place for their family, then he'd come home soon and it would be settled.

"Lord, I believe You are telling us to move to Jamaica, but have you seen those ugly filthy places with the high priced rent which we cannot afford? And the crime rate is at an all time high, so You wouldn't want me and Emily to be in that kind of dangerous place, would You?" Grace said, arguing with God.

As God continually brought back the same vision both she and Chris had in that local church, Grace knew she was in trouble but she still continued to try and bargain with God.

"Okay, God, if you really want me to move there, let me tell you what I'd want in the house. I'd like to have a large English style kitchen. We will need to cook a lot since it is not so safe there to eat out. And we would need at least four bedrooms upstairs, one for Emily, one for us, one for guest room, and one for a playroom so we can have a safe environment for Emily to have other children come to play in. All this needs to be under $1,300 (USD) a month in order for us to comfortably afford it. If it happens, then I know for sure it's Your will for us to relocate there."

Grace was so confident that it would not happen and was not surprised when Chris emailed her that all he found after a day of searching was, "Another ugly house." She told no one, not even her husband, of her request.

One day Chris emailed Grace and attached several more photos than usual. The first photo was of him standing in front of a large house. He looked so small compared to it that Grace thought that they might have rooms for rent in a house that big. The second and third photos were of what Chris described as an English style kitchen that was too big to fit into one photo. The next photo was from the upstairs looking down. In the description, Chris said there were six bedrooms! The final photo was a large beautiful garden. By then Grace's jaw had dropped, but she reasoned, "Well, the price couldn't be cheap. It must be way over our budget."

In the final sentence of the email, Chris said that the landlord had listed the classified ad in the newspaper in Jamaican currency last month, and since the Jamaican currency collapsed last week, now the rental was only $1,100 (USD) a month. It was well within their budget! Grace sat at her mother-in-law's laptop crying as she read the email over and over again.

"Another ugly house?" Chris' mother asked as she entered the room. "It's okay, Grace. I am sure he'll find a decent one soon."

"See for yourself," Grace said, sliding the laptop toward her.

After reading the email, Chris mother said with a smile, "It's incredible!"

"I know!" exclaimed Grace.

"So…why are you crying?" her mother-in-law asked.

"I'm just speechless!" Grace said as she marveled at how God had given her everything she'd asked for and more. But why was she surprised? She knew she should be used to it by now.

Ask Yourself

- Have you ever relocated to different city, state, or country? If yes, how was the adjustment process for you?
- Have you ever prayed the kind of specific prayer Grace did and gotten it answered?
- What do you think of the relationship between Grace and God?

Chapter 13

Living in an Under-developed Country

L ife in Jamaica was very different from life in Switzerland or Asia. Grace did not realize how many things she had taken for granted before and quickly found that normal, every-day things in Europe and Asia were considered luxury items in Jamaica. Grace and Chris had to buy a year's worth of baby supplies before moving because they were so highly priced in Jamaica. Utilities were also very expensive. Grace could not often make calls to her family overseas, and the few times she was able to, she could not talk for very long. Seems this was typical when you lived in an under-developed country like Jamaica.

The hot and humid tropical climate was another thing Grace and her family needed to get used to, especially when the power supply was not guaranteed for daily life. Almost every other day, Grace experienced the power shortage situation where it would be shut off during the hottest hours of the day in residential areas in order to conserve power for the resorts. While power was shut off, it meant no water, no fan, and no air conditioning. Grace would sit in a rocking chair in Emily's room and try to get Emily to take a nap, but with the intense heat and extreme humidity it became impossible to be comfortable even while doing nothing.

Grace became very close with many of the women in the neighborhood a majority of their husbands worked at the same hotel as Chris, and they were all foreigners. The locals thought they were strange and often did not associate with them. In the grocery store, Grace became accustomed to getting strange glances from people. Due to the extreme poverty in the area, she was warned by others never to go grocery shopping alone, and be prepared to be robbed for as little as five dollars. Grace began to carry two wallets. One was a real one with important items in it, and the other she used as a fake so that she could toss it away to buy some time to get away as the robbers chased it. She could see it wasn't normally a case where those people necessarily wanted to harm her; they just desperately needed the money.

Clearly security was an issue in Jamaica. Though the area in which Grace lived was safe in general, outside their residential area danger lurked on every road, in every alley, and at every street corner. The roads were bumpy and full of potholes. Whenever it rained (which happened often) the holes would fill up with water, and become difficult to see. Cars would often drive over them and get flat tires. But Grace learned from her neighborhood friends that if she was ever to get a flat tire, she should never stop until she knew she was in a safe, public place to avoid possible danger.

It had been a humbling experience for Grace as she went from a self-sufficient, confident career woman, to a housewife depending on her husband in Switzerland, and then into her new role of motherhood. Just when she finally settled down and got comfortable with what

Switzerland had to offer, she found herself relocated to this under-developed country where most everything was perceived as a "luxury," even her family's safety.

The Safety Issue

The house which God provided for them to rent was located in a relatively safe area. Yet the windows of all the houses had bars on the inside to prevent crimes. It made Grace feel like a prisoner in her own home. The soaring crime rate constantly put everyone on edge and brought great stress to Grace. She hoped God would not keep them here too long. She didn't like the thought of raising a family in a place where there was no peace, due to the constant fear of being hurt or robbed.

As the unemployment rate soared to 25% in Jamaica, Grace observed that it seemed the women would work harder than most of the men. It was quite normal to see women with several children, each from a different father. Since the women worked very hard to provide for their families, it made them demanding and tough.

One day, Elaina, the wife of the baker working in the same hotel as Chris phoned Grace obviously in a panic, "Grace! I need help!"

"Where are you, are you okay?" Grace sensed something was very wrong and knew Elaina's husband was out of the town on a business trip.

"I'll explain later, can you come to pick me up at the McDonald's, please!" begged Elaina.

"Sure, I will be there in five minutes," Grace responded, relieved to know at least Elaina was in a safe public place.

Grace hurriedly placed Emily in the car, and called Chris at work to let him know where she would be. Moments later, she arrived at McDonald's and anxiously searched the eating area for Elaina, who she finally saw was waving to her from the very back corner of the store. As she got closer to Elaina, Grace's jaw dropped when she saw there were many bruises on Elaina's beautiful face, a few of them were covered over with dried blood. Elaina was trying to breathe evenly as she tried to calm her own three-year-old boy. He was happy to see Emily which allowed Grace to speak quietly with Elaina. She looked like she'd just gone through hell.

"What happened?" Grace asked with deep concern in her voice.

The tears came as Elaina looked to the floor. The emotions she had apparently been trying to keep under control suddenly exploded into helpless sobbing. Grace just let her release her emotions as she tried to shield Elaina from the eyes of the other patrons in the store.

"We were robbed!" Elaina was finally able to tell Grace. "After I came home from grocery shopping, I entered through our front door. I placed everything in the kitchen and then all of the sudden, from out of nowhere, a big man, grabbed my boy and placed his knife on my boy's neck."

Grace was speechless.

"I didn't care about myself, I was afraid for my son. I jumped on the man and tried to get my boy out of his hand. He hit me back hard and I fell to the floor!" Elaina said, clenching her fists with anger. "He came at me with the knife and asked for money!"

As Elaine paused to take a drink, Grace asked, "So you gave him some?"

"I told him I would but I needed to get to my purse which was on the other side of the room. He grabbed me by the hair and walked me toward to my handbag. Then he started touching me in an evil way!"

"Oh, no..." Grace gasped in horror.

"I know!" Elaina cried, "I suddenly realized he might have other motives as well. There were millions of thoughts running through my mind, but my priority was keeping my son safe. As I opened the handbag, I grabbed my pepper spray. I sprayed a good dose right in his face and as soon as he let go of my hair, I grabbed my son and took off running. I didn't stop until I got here!"

As Elaina paused to take a deep breath, Grace asked, "Did you call the police?"

"I surely did, but you know they hardly move, especially for foreigners," Elaina said angrily.

Amazed, Grace asked, "What did they say?"

"They said robbery is quite normal around here and told me to stop showing off my stuff. They told me I should behave myself in public and then things like this wouldn't happen," Elaina said as the tears threatened to start again.

"What?" Grace responded angrily, she couldn't believe what Elaina had just told her.

"Grace, I hate this place, I want to go home!" Elaina cried again.

"You mean go back to France?" Grace asked remembering that was where Elaina had said they were from.

"Yes, go back to France, or anywhere else," Elaina declared, "Anywhere would be better than here!"

Grace brought Elaina and her son home with her. When Chris came home, they brought the issue to the hotel management, and few weeks later, Elaina and her family moved back to France. The incident left an invisible scar in everyone's mind, especially Grace.

Since safety was such an issue, most of these foreigners couldn't do much outdoor activities. The "highlight of the week" came whenever they took turns hosting a gathering so their children could have safe play dates. They would cook and share interesting stories with each other. As most of these families came from America, Grace often just sat there and listened to them talking about the way things were in the USA. They also often talked about the medical facility here on the island and how it was not well equipped at all. They told Grace that when any of them got close to the last stages of pregnancy, they would go back to America to deliver the baby. Grace pondered all that she heard as she attempted to adjust to this often unsafe environment.

Other Cultural Adjustments

It was difficult to adjust to such a difference in culture and economy. Good produce was scarce and expensive, as were many other fresh products. Although the soil was very rich and fairly easy to grow produce in, Grace quickly discovered that the Jamaican people did not like to farm. It reminded them of when they were enslaved by the British. Grace thought that a bit absurd since they would benefit very much from farming and it would help then rise above their severe poverty level.

There was one woman, Jackie, who did grow her own produce. It was the freshest around. Everyone would go to her. The prices were a bit higher than the produce at the grocery store, but her products were by far the best. All the foreigners loved to purchase from her and Grace was one of her more frequent customers.

"Good morning, Ms. Grace!" Jackie greeted her in her regular joyful voice.

"Hey, Jackie! How are you?" Grace responded as she stepped into Jackie's little "store" (a tent to be exact) where she displayed all her fresh vegetables.

"I am doing good, business is good. Are you cooking for the crowd tonight again?" Jackie asked with a big grin on her face.

"Yes," Grace laughed, "I think my home has become a 'Chinese restaurant,' except they don't pay."

There were no "safe" restaurants nearby except for the ones in the hotels. There were a few McDonalds' around but robbers would even wait outside these places so people were afraid to go there. Grace's kitchen had become one of the favorites places for this community to gather. Every other day it seemed she would have at least ten people coming over for dinner. Grace loved it though; it was the perfect opportunity for her to share God's love with them.

On Sundays, she and her family still went to the same church they had visited before they moved there. It blessed Grace to see her daughter playing and getting along with the local children. She wished she could take her daughter to play with other children on a regular basis, but it was just too dangerous.

In May of 2001, Grace found out she was pregnant with their second child. Chris and Grace were very happy and always liked the idea of having two children. However, Jamaica's medical facility was a concern for them. Grace was due for her first prenatal check-up so she made an appointment at the local facility. When she and Chris stepped into the dimly lit waiting room, Grace looked around to see there were hardly any men in the waiting room. Most of the expectant moms were there alone. Grace tried to calm herself as she looked for a clean place to sit. She looked at the dirty floor, dusty curtains, and the sticky substance on the sofa. She was still wondering whether to sit or not when the nurse appeared from behind a squeaky door and called her name.

Chris and Grace followed the nurse into the "doctor's office" where there was a simple wooden desk piled high with papers and documents. There were two chairs, a white curtain fixed on some iron bar that seemed to serve as partition, and then a bed behind it. Grace and Chris stood looking nervously at each other, not quite sure what to expect.

Moments later, a female doctor entered the room, introduced herself as Dr. Smith and invited Grace and Chris to sit in the empty chairs.

As Grace sat down in front of one of the "paper mountains" and to her horror she saw a line of ants crawling across the papers. Though the rest of the visit went okay, Grace and Chris were glad to leave that office. Grace felt extremely uncomfortable lying on that bed, concerned about the lack of basic hygiene even in the doctor's office.

As the days went by, Grace found herself often looking towards to the sky and praying, "God, I know you hear me, I am getting anxious about things. I trust You know I have been trying to do my best to adjust to the life here. People think I am crazy when I share my faith stories with them. They enjoy my Chinese food, but not what You have to offer them."

Tears streaming down her face, Grace poured her heart out to God, "Now I am pregnant with our second child. You know that the medical facility here is not ideal. I am quite scared from time to time. I often think of Elaina, and the other recent robbery cases I have heard about. Lord, I feel I am living in a prison behind all these metal bars everyday. I know You have some purpose for us here, but I also know You don't mind if I tell you what I feel! Father, please tell me what else You want me to do here. I sense it's time for us to move on before I give birth to this precious child but I don't want to be separated from my husband like so many other couples have done. It's not right for a husband and wife to be apart for months at a time, especially at the time of the birth of their child."

The Gunshot!

One night, as Grace was preparing dinner, Chris called her to let her know he would be home from work in a half hour. Thirty minutes later there was no sign of Chris. "He must just be running a bit late," thought Grace, "he'll be home soon." But thirty minutes turned into an hour and still Chris was not home. Nervous, Grace called the hotel to ask where he was. The manager said they looked around but could not find him. As Grace hung up the phone, her heart was beating very fast. What if something happened to him? It wasn't like him to be late and not call her. Suddenly, Grace heard gunshots outside in the immediate neighborhood. She froze!

"Lord, I know You didn't bring us this far to just drop us off! Wherever Chris is now, please protect him and bring him safely home, thank You, Lord!" Grace prayed urgently.

After three long hours of frantic worrying, Grace finally heard the front door open. She rushed to the door to see Chris standing there. His suit jacket was off and his tie was undone. His white shirt was stained with mud and he looked worn out and tired. Grace ran to him and hugged him. Moments later she pulled away and stood glaring at him.

"Where on earth have you been?" she asked angrily, tears streaming down her face.

"I'm sorry. I got delayed. The car got a flat tire and a nice gentleman helped me repair it. It took two hours just to get the tire off," chuckling slightly as he remembered the incident.

"Neither of us could get it," he tried to explain as laughter overtook him. "At one point we both just stood back and stared at it as if we were two monkeys trying to figure out what to do with one banana."

Red with rage Grace yelled, "You think this is funny? Do you have any idea how worried I've been? You could have at least called me!"

Chris immediately stopped laughing suddenly realizing how upset Grace really was, "I couldn't. My phone died. I wanted to call you, but honestly I've been fine. I never wanted you to worry."

"Well, what was I supposed to do? Just sit here and not worry that my husband hasn't been home for hours and nobody knows where he is? Am I not supposed to care that something terrible could have happened…that those gunshots I heard outside could mean that I would be left to raise two children on my own? How could you expect me not to worry when we…" Grace's voice trailed off as she went into the kitchen sobbing.

Chris followed her, "When we what?"

"When we live in a place like this!" Grace screamed out, letting loose all her pent up emotions.

"What do you mean by that?" Chris asked, wondering how the conversation had gotten so out of hand.

"You know exactly what I mean! Look around! All this poverty and crime – I can't take it anymore!" Grace said crying hysterically now, "I hate it here! This is no place to raise a family."

Chris embraced her trying to calm and reassure her, "I know it's hard here, but we've done pretty well this long haven't we? I admit this isn't exactly an ideal place to live, but we have it good here. Besides, where else would we go?"

Just then another gunshot split the air. This time, both of them heard it. They looked at each other, nerves on edge.

"Back to Switzerland, Asia, even America," Grace said frantically, "Anywhere. Just please not here. We can't live like this. Please, please let's go somewhere else."

"Alright," Chris calmly replied, "I'll put in a request at work to be transferred as soon as possible."

In the next few weeks Chris did as he had promised and asked to be transferred out of Jamaica. His general manager suggested he send a request to their new sister hotel in Sarasota, Florida. After a few phone interviews, Chris was hired by this soon to be opening sister hotel.

September, 2001

It was the first week of September 2001 that they packed up their belongings and returned their house back to the landlord. They checked into the hotel where Chris was still working for their last week in Jamaica. All they had left to do was have their final meeting with the

US Embassy in Jamaica so they could pick up their approved visas and relocate to Florida, USA. The day before they had planned to leave for the embassy, Grace was feeding Emily when her room phone rang. It was Martha, a lovely lady Grace had become close friends with.

"Grace, turn on the TV now!" Martha said with high-pitch voice.

"What's going on, are you okay, Martha?" Grace asked as she tried to find the TV remote while holding the phone.

"Go to the CNN channel," Martha urged her.

"Oh my God! Grace, did you see that? The Twin Towers are gone!" Martha screamed.

Grace's jaw dropped! This was not a movie! It was the real Twin Towers! The screen showed a man covered with ashes assisting a woman walking and holding a mask to her face, and many more people were covered by ashes. Then the "re-play" of the aircrafts flying into the towers drove Grace to her knees! "No, Lord! No, God! This is your beloved nation!"

Chris learned that their appointment with the embassy and their flight to Sarasota, Florida had been cancelled. Everything had to be postponed as the US Homeland Security Department tightened security everywhere.

During this time, Grace began to have some irregular bleeding and anxiously checked with the local doctor. She really wasn't much help but advised Grace to calm down and take it easy. With everything up in the air, nobody could tell them what would happen next. They could only wait and pray! It took six weeks but they finally received their visas and were ready to relocate to U.S.A.

Ask Yourself

- Can you think of something in your life which you might be taking for granted like the lack of power for her utilities that Grace experienced in Jamaica?

- What do you think was going on in Grace's mind when she heard what happened to her friend, Elaina?

- Why do you think Grace was angry at Chris when he was casual about his unexpected delay in getting home that night?

- Have you ever relied on working visas to stay in a foreign country? Can you relate to the feelings of Chris and Grace as their entry to USA was delayed?

Chapter 14

Fighting for Baby's Life

R ight after landing in Sarasota, FL, the hotel assisted them in renting a temporary fully furnished apartment for a month while they looked for a long term leasing property. Chris' working hours were very demanding as it was a pre-opening for this hotel. He had so much to do that he sometimes had to stay overnight to finish the tasks. The exhaustion of Grace's physical condition as she entered her last stages of pregnancy, and Chris' long hours working added some serious challenges to their quest for new housing. After two weeks of house hunting, they still hadn't found anything they felt comfortable settling their family into.

One night, after a particularly trying day for both of them, they went down on their knees and cried out to God, "Father, we thank You for bringing us here and giving us a safer environment for our family. Lord, you know we need to find a house which we feel at peace with so please guide us to the right house tomorrow, in Jesus' name, we pray! Amen!"

The following day they followed up on a newspaper ad and met with the landlord of the rental, a lovely lady named Debbie.

"So what do you think?" Debbie asked after she took them through the house.

"I must say it's very spacious, and looks very new!" Chris commented.

"Do you know of any churches close by in this neighborhood?" Grace asked.

Debbie's eyes registered surprise, "Why, yes, what kind of church are you looking for?"

"A non-denominational, spirit-led church that stresses a deep relationship with God, not religion," Grace replied firmly.

Debbie smiled broadly, "Then I can introduce you guys to my home church!"

"Really? That would be awesome!" Grace responded, thankful for how God had led them to this house and to meet Debbie.

After they signed the lease for the house, they were still waiting for their belongings to arrive via overseas cargo from Jamaica. They were happy to find they would still be able to stay in the current fully-furnished apartment until their belongings arrived. However, while they still had two weeks to go on the current lease, they received a phone call saying they needed to be out by the end of the week, because the landlord himself needed the room to attend a conference in town, and he couldn't find a hotel room to book.

"Please, Mr. Fred," Grace pleaded with him, "Our furniture and belongings haven't arrived yet. How can we find another place in such short amount of time? Besides we are talking about a whole family with one young child, and one is on the way. Would you please consider some other options?"

"Well, it's not my problem. I am operating my million-dollar business here. I tried but the whole town is booked! Since our contract is only good for thirty days, and the contract allows either side to terminate it anytime within those thirty days, I suggest you go find a place before this Friday," he said as he hung up, obviously unmoved by Grace's plea!

"Father God, did I miss something here? Why doesn't it ever seem to become easier for us in this journey?" Grace prayed as tears ran down on her cheeks.

Seeing her tears, three-year-old Emily ran to give her mother a hug.

"Mama, are you okay? You wanna play with me?" Emily placed her little hands around Grace's face.

"Emily, Mama is fine," Grace assured her daughter, "I'll play with you a bit later, okay? Let me make a few more phone calls first."

Grace called Debbie for help, and asked if they could move in two weeks early.

"Of course," she said, "But you know there is no furniture or anything currently in there."

"We know," Grace acknowledged, then added sadly, "We don't have much choice here."

Grace hesitated but decided to ask, " I know this is big favor to ask, especially since we don't know each other much yet, Debbie, but do you have any spare blankets and mattress we can borrow for these next two weeks? Since the flooring is mostly tile, it would help us to sleep better."

"Oh, Grace, bless your heart! Let me see what I can do. I think we might have a few sleeping bags around the house. There's no way for you with that big tummy to lay on those cold hard floors. Let me see what I can do and I'll call you back," Debbie said with compassion.

"Thank you so much, Debbie! You are God-sent!" Grace said but this time the tears she was shedding were of joy not sadness.

By end of the week, they moved into their new home. With no furniture, no chairs, no bed, no nothing. Debbie found two sets of sleeping bags for Grace and Emily, while Chris stayed overnight at the hotel; which was in its last stage of Grand Opening preparation. Grace and Emily slept on the floor at night and played there during the day as well, since there was no furniture to sit on. "It's okay, we can make it through this," Grace thought to herself, "at least we are in the much safer environment for our family."

Their furniture and belongings arrived and Grace was glad to finally be settling in as her second child would soon be born. Several weeks before her due date, Grace had an ultrasound. Afterwards, the three doctors who were in charge of her case informed her that there was a high possibility that the child would have spinal defects and Downs Syndrome. The doctors recommended a specific amniocentesis test for Grace to take so they could further prove whether their diagnosis was accurate.

"What are the side effects of this particular test?" Grace asked.

"Well, according to the stats, after an amniocentesis women may experience cramping, bleeding, or leaking of amniotic fluid. There is also a slight risk of infection. The risk of miscarriage is about one in 200 after an amniocentesis in the second trimester of pregnancy," one of the doctors said.

"One in 200!" Grace replied, shocked by this information, "So why should I take this risk?"

"So you can have options," another doctor answered.

"What kind of options do you mean?" Graced asked wondering where this conversation was headed.

"If the results of the test confirm what we think and your baby does have a spinal defect or Downs Syndrome, then you can consider whether to end the pregnancy," the third doctor explained.

Grace couldn't quite comprehend what she just heard. "Did he just say abort my baby?!" she thought.

"So, if I have no intention of aborting the baby, then I don't have to take the test, right?" Grace asked.

"Well, you really should consider an abortion," replied one of the doctors, "because this child would only be a burden to you and to society."

"I don't want to abort my child," Grace declared obstinately.

"I really think you should consider having this procedure done," said another doctor.

"Well, I don't want to be that one in 200 percentile you spoke of that suffers one of the side effects," Grace declared, her voice rising to a higher octave.

"Madame, the odds of that happening are highly unlikely," one doctor said trying to calm her down.

"But you want me to abort the baby anyway so what's the difference?" Grace asked angrily.

The doctors continued to debate with Grace until she was in tears. She called her husband at work and explained the entire situation to him. After three hours of "negotiating," the doctors finally gave up. Grace went home very upset, but not before having to sign a document stating that it was her decision not to take the test and not the doctors' responsibility if the child was born with any birth defects.

At church that Sunday, Grace found comfort in speaking to several women who had all been through similar situations. They shared story after story of their miracle babies. Grace was very thankful for God's love shown through these ladies. The women didn't stop there, they even asked her if they could organize a baby shower for her.

"What is a baby shower?" Grace asked one of the ladies.

In Asia, it was only after the baby was born that loved ones would bring gifts. Here, the custom seemed to be quite the opposite.

"All you have to do," one of the women explained, "is go down to the stores you like, and write down what you want. Then bring us the list and we'll go get those things for you."

This was quite a foreign concept for Grace. She had never done anything like this before in her life, but it blessed her very much. She found herself being so loved by these new friends. As time went on, this group of women continued to stand with Grace in faith and prayer for the baby. Grace was very grateful for their support on what would have been another lonely journey.

Only a couple short weeks later, the baby was born. Much to Grace and Chris's relief, their son, Peter, was healthy and had no spinal defects or Downs Syndrome. They gave God all the thanks and all the glory for their healthy baby boy. However, several months passed and Grace noticed that Peter's gross motor development was extremely slow. He had not attempted to move around much even at six months old. Grace and Chris became concerned and decided to take him to a doctor. After a series of tests the doctors said they did not know what was wrong with him and recommended a therapist. The therapist they hired just "happened to be" a Christian woman who did home therapy. She spent an hour and a half working with Peter once a week for several weeks.

When she finished her final session and did her analysis, she said to Grace, "Your son is fine. He's just being a lazy boy. He won't go and get the things he wants because he'd rather you go get it and bring it to him. Just don't give in to his cries when he wants something that's well within his reach. Once he tries he'll find he can do it by himself."

Grace was encouraged by these words and once again grateful that there was nothing majorly wrong with her son. Several weeks later, the family travelled back to Switzerland to visit Chris's parents for Christmas. Grace had missed the snow-capped mountains more than she'd realized. One afternoon while Grace, Chris, and Emily—who was now almost four—went out skiing with Chris's father, Peter was left in his grandmother's care. Most of the day he simply lay in the middle of the living room floor, apparently interested in watching the dog who was laying just a few feet away. Chris's mother went into the kitchen for a moment leaving Peter lying in the middle of the room. Moments later when she returned, she saw that he had scooted himself over to reach the dog. She could not believe it! The moment the rest of the family returned, she immediately relayed to Grace what had happened.

"All right, he's showing some progress," Grace said with a happy grin.

After a lovely week in Switzerland, the family returned to Florida. Everything seemed to be going great. They had just taken a wonderful vacation, Peter was finally moving, and Chris had recently been promised a promotion at the hotel. The week following their return, Chris learned that the hotel had hired someone new to fill the position he had been promised. It was a huge disappointment for Chris and Grace, as they had been looking forward to it for quite a while.

That night, as he and Grace discussed the situation, Grace found herself very upset. She did not understand why her husband did not get the position he had been promised; especially after he had done all the extra duties they'd asked him to in the last eight months!

In her devotional time, Grace talked this over with God, "Lord, it's not fair! Have you seen how they treated Chris?"

As Grace wrote her feelings out in her journal, she was led to read **Psalm 37:34.** *"Hope in the LORD and keep his way. He will exalt you to inherit the land; when the wicked are destroyed, you will see it."*

In the same week, both Grace and Chris kept getting the Bible story about "Joseph" and the journey he had after being sold by his own brothers to becoming the person in charge in Egypt. There were many bumpy roads in between but he always knew God was with him.

"Lord, what are you saying?" Grace prayed.

"Are you ready to go to your Promised Land?" Grace felt God asking her.

"Lord, I guess that means there might be something else You want to show me about the journey?" Grace wrote in her journal.

"Before the [Promised Land], you will need to go through [Egypt] first," Grace continued to journal down what she felt God was saying in her heart.

"Lord, so are You saying soon You are leading us to our [Egypt]?" Grace asked.

"Oh, that's just great! That's exactly what I needed to hear from you, Lord!" Grace complained in her heart. Moments later, Grace sensed such a conviction within her, "Father, I am sorry, I know You can see the whole picture, and I can't." She submitted and relinquished control to God once again.

Later that week, the general manager from the Michigan location contacted Chris and offered him the same position there, but with much lower pay. After talking to God, they agreed to go to the interview. Grace knew that this was the "Egypt" God had been talking about. Within a few short days all the arrangements had been made for Chris to begin working there. He would start at the end of the month. Grace was not particularly excited about moving again, but there was unspeakable peace in their hearts, she knew this was God's will. She had given Him full control.

Ask Yourself

- What are your thoughts about Grace's decision to refuse the test which the three doctors insisted she have before the birth of her second child?

- Have you ever felt "cheated" or "betrayed" at the work place? How do you deal with it?

- Will you follow God when it is not convenient, even to the point of going to "Egypt"?

Chapter 15

Getting into the "Egypt Encounter" With God

I n Michigan, they put Emily in public school. She seemed to like it there until Christmas time came and she was told that she could not speak about God or about Jesus' birth. Upon hearing of this, Grace scheduled a meeting with Emily's teacher.

"I myself am a Christian," the teacher said, "and I've tried to talk about angels and things of God to give the children a sense of what Christmas is really about, but each time I've been firmly scolded by other staff members and even by the principle. I cannot talk about God, and I cannot let our students talk about Him either."

"I see," Grace said, "Well, that's unfortunate because I don't want my daughter to be in a suppressed environment where she is not free to speak about the Lord."

Grace spoke with the principle as well and then they decided to take Emily out of the school. They soon found a private Christian school for her, but it was in the next town.

White Christmas

That year Grace had another white Christmas. She had missed the snow very much. The first night it snowed, they were all very excited for some of their fonder memories of Switzerland were of the snow. The next day, however, as Chris opened the garage to go to work, he was met with a snow-covered driveway. In Switzerland the government would clear the roads and driveways of snow so the locals could move freely about the city. But they discovered to their distress that in Michigan they had to do it themselves. Chris let out a heavy sigh as he went back inside, changed his clothes, then he and Grace grabbed the shovels. They spent the entire morning shoveling snow from the driveway.

Of course Emily wanted to help, too. In her puffy winter coat, she vigorously plunged her tiny shovel into the mounds of snow. As she tried to lift it out of the snow, she realized it was too heavy. Removing the shovel from the snow, she tried again on the other side of the driveway. Again, her strength failed her. After several frustrating and fruitless attempts, she finally gave up and began rolling around and making snow angels. Her parents chuckled as they watched.

Things seemed to be going smoothly for the first month or two. Emily liked her school, things were going well with Chris's job, and Grace enjoyed the peace in the house during the day as she took care of Peter.

Activating the Gifts

Over the next couple of months, the family had visited several churches but had not found any they felt was the one they were to attend. They were running out of options for churches in their small town of Livonia. One Sunday they decided to visit a church in Detroit. Detroit was not the best area of Michigan, but they did not mind going there if they found a church they liked. They did like the small church they found which had only about 300-400 people in the congregation. It was a strong apostolic, international church. The pastors were Caucasian but most of the congregation were a combination of many different nation-alities. Grace and her family found themselves at home there. Grace liked their worship very much. They did a lot of prophetic dancing and had ribbons laid out at the front of the stage for the children to wave during the songs. Grace felt the Spirit of God so strongly that it reminded her of her old church back in Taipei.

After attending the church for several weeks, Grace decided she wanted to participate in the upcoming women's conference. She knew it was going to be powerful. As she prayed about it, she asked that everything she was going to hear from God during the conference, Chris would hear also.

Chris had just begun to experience Grace's prophetic gift. Grace was able to tell something about each person she met within the first few moments of meeting them. When she and Chris were first introduced to the hotel chef by Chris's general manager, Grace could immediately tell that the chef did not respect women. Upon sharing this with her husband, he was confused as to why she would make such an accusa-tion and did not believe her. Three months later, the chef was fired for sexual harassment. Chris felt a bit embarrassed as he relayed the news to Grace realizing her suspicion about the man was correct. Knowing that her husband probably did not know what to make of her strong spiritual connection, she felt strongly that they needed to be united in their faith and prayed for Chris to be able to receive from God the same things she did, so God could become even more real to him.

Through Egypt

In January of 2004, before she headed out to the women's conference, Grace opened a brand new journal and wrote:

"Lord, I believe You brought us here for very specific purposes, and I trust one is to strengthen our marriage even more, and that includes Chris having a closer relationship with you and more alert to your Spirit inside of him. Father, as I am attending this conference, I pray that You will not only speak to me, You will somehow speak to Chris as well. As husband and wife are one, whatever I receive here in this conference Chris will receive it, too. One more thing, Lord, I know I haven't been journaling much these past few years and I've really missed the time we communicate through my journaling time. Please forgive me, Father, as I start this New Year journaling again. In Jesus' name I pray, Amen!"

In the afternoon during the one-on-one prayer session, Grace was standing with three pastors and asked to be prayed for without telling them any details of what she had been praying for. Grace was waiting for a confirmation from God. What God inspired them to pray was so powerful that Grace was grateful it was recorded on tape so she was able to review it later:

My hands are upon you, My hands are upon you. I have set your life as a map. You have asked Me to show you the next page so you would know what's next as I have moved you here and there...I say to you: "Trust in Me, trust in Me. Each place you go, come with an open heart and an open bag to receive." Each time as I moved you from place to place, you have gone with greater treasure, greater treasure. You know in your heart that the call on your life is truly to be used as a minister of the gospel. I have heard your heart's cry as you have prayed: "Lord, I just want to settle in and build a work for You."

Do not despair, I am doing some temporary things here and there; they are not fruitless, nor are they little. They are valuable. Things are taking place behind the scenes. This is not your settled place yet, I still have one more place to move you to. So don't despair. Allow your heart to be connected with the ones that are here and keep your life open to receive.

And even I speak to you, Son! And you said: "Lord, You moved me here and there, but I don't see the advancement. I keep making the move, but it doesn't advance me in the places I sensed to go." But Son, the day of promotion is coming! The day of promotion is coming! Know that you have been developing a reputation, you will be known as a man of integrity, a man to be trusted, a man to be depended upon, and when My timing is right, you are not just to move up one step or two, but three. You will move up to be greatly advanced! You'll see the increase; you'll see the opportunity to truly establish your family. Then you will begin to see how I'm going to use you to plant My Kingdom in places that no other ones have the opportunity to go.

For Son, you will have the opportunity to speak to those who are high up in the business and financial realms. You'll have opportunities to connect with CEOs, and those ones with prestigious positions, and you will become the one that they trust. You will be able to feed them My Word, pray over them, see their families set free and delivered. And you will see My purpose advanced and you will truly be My Kingdom builder.

And Daughter, as I am advancing you as a Kingdom builder, I am also advancing you through the ideas in your journaling time. Those fresh ideas for ministries, Daughter, just continue to share with Me in your journal, share your thoughts with Me and I will begin to move on them! For truly I have planted them in your heart and you will see them come true, saith the Lord.

Grace fell on her knees and sobbed in awe of how God answered her prayers in such a detailed way! From her heart cry about Chris' burden to her picking up journaling again. As one of the pastors gave her the recorded tape, she knew she had one of the most valuable treasures of all right in hand—the Word of God! Grace couldn't wait to go home and shared everything with Chris!

God's Promotion

As they continued to walk in faith, the time came for them to renew their work visas. Though Grace knew God was at work in their lives, they were still having complications with their visas and would soon have to make a decision to either move out of the country for a year or Chris would have to find another job.

As they were praying about their work situation, an international minister whom Grace followed and admired for years came to Michigan to conduct a conference. Grace was so excited to be able to meet him in person. When she arrived for the first day of the three-day conference, she found the venue packed with over 5,000 people in attendance! Grace had to take a seat in the back section of the seating and still experienced the presence of God so strong that she began to speak in tongues. She was amazed! She had never done that before.

After worship on the second day of the conference, the minister prayed and opened the Bible. But before he began to read, he asked anyone in the building who was waiting for a job promotion to stand up. Grace and Chris had been waiting for the promised promotion for almost six months. She immediately felt tears begin to run down her face as she stood for Chris. Even though he was at work, Grace knew God considered husband and wife as one. There were only a few others who stood as she anxiously waited to hear what the minster would say next. As he glanced around at those standing, he reassured them that God said their promotion was coming. Grace was so relieved to hear those words.

They had been waiting for the promotion for so long she had begun to doubt it would ever come.

As they waited to see what God had in mind for Chris, his general manager offered to help Chris apply at a location out of the country so they might obtain a visa to come back to the U.S.A. later.

When Chris refused, the general manager asked, "Well, do you at least have a back-up plan?"

"I don't need a back-up plan," Chris replied, "this was God's will. He will provide."

When Chris told Grace about the conversation with his general manager, she praised God knowing her husband's faith had truly been strengthened. The following month, Chris got a phone call from Tim, a man he used to work with back in Sarasota. Tim had gotten promoted to hotel manager in the Las Vegas location. He was looking for a Food and Beverage Director. This could be the promotion Chris had been waiting for! Excitedly he agreed to go to an interview. After ending the phone call with Tim, Chris immediately called Grace. She was in the middle of cooking some dumplings and watching Peter playing on the floor when the phone rang.

Chris's voice seemed very loud and excited, "I got it! I got the opportunity of promotion!"

Grace had never heard him so excited and her heart leapt with happiness as she let out a shout of joy and said, "This is so wonderful!"

"I know!" Chris continued, "It's at a new location."

"Where?" Grace asked, anxious to hear what God had done.

"Las Vegas," Chris replied, "It's one of the best places for someone in the Food and Beverage field in the world!"

"Oh, this must be an attack of the devil!" said Grace emphatically, quickly rebuking the enemy and did not hear Chris as he tried to reason with her.

"Just go look up the hotel on the internet. It's not even really in Las Vegas. It's in Henderson, which is right outside of Vegas," Chris tried to explain.

"Honey, are you out of your mind, what shall we do in Vegas with our two young children?" Grace protested.

Still convinced that this was the enemy trying to trick them and throw them off the right track, Grace refused and hung up the phone. Suddenly, she heard the Holy Spirit ask her sternly what she was thinking.

"Didn't I tell you the promotion is coming?" Grace felt God impress upon her heart.

"Yes, You did, Lord; but it's in Sin City, the capitol of casinos, what would we be doing there as a family?"

Startled, Grace dropped her spatula and ended up burning her dumplings. Embarrassed, she quickly repented for not yielding to God's plan, then went to the computer and looked up the hotel just as her husband had requested. It looked like the city of Henderson was a very family friendly place after all.

In April of 2004, they made a four-day trip to Las Vegas for the interview. They stayed in a lovely suite at the hotel. As they checked in, Grace opened the curtains and she saw the beautiful desert mountains.

She'd never seen mountains like these before, except in pictures. She was reminded of God's majesty as she gazed upon the landscape.

While she stood in front of the large window, she heard God's voice, "Grace, do you remember the scriptures of Mark 11:22-24?"

"Yes, Lord, I recall what those verses are about," she said and then she quoted them in her heart from memory.

"Have faith in God," Jesus answered. "Truly I tell you, if anyone says to this mountain, 'Go, throw yourself into the sea,' and does not doubt in their heart but believes that what they say will happen, it will be done for them. Therefore I tell you, whatever you ask for in prayer, believe that you have received it, and it will be yours."

"Good, you will need it very soon," Grace felt God impressing upon her mind.

Four days had gone by, the interview could not have gone better! Chris had signed the contract and everything seemed to be going according to plan. Before they left, however, they decided to take a drive down the Las Vegas strip which they had heard so much about. Exiting the elevator, they walked towards the lobby door when they were stopped by Tim and the Human Resources Director. They had just found out that Chris and Grace's current visas would not work out. It was like a bomb had just gone off in their world and their hearts sank from the impact of it. Standing in the middle of the lobby, devastated by what they had just been told, Grace looked at Chris hoping he could figure out a way to fix this. She suddenly heard God's voice once again bring Mark 11:22-24 to her remembrance.

"Please excuse us for a few moments," Grace said as she grabbed Chris by the arm and pulled him toward the elevator.

On the way back up to their room, Grace told Chris, "There are some verses I need to read. God told me to remember them because I was going to need them soon. If ever I needed those verses, it's now."

As they made their way back to the room, Chris was silent as he tried to process what had just happened. Grace immediately went to her Bible, looked up the verses in Mark and read them aloud so her husband could hear. Then they knelt together in front of the bed and began to pray. They refused to let this visa complication get in the way of God's plan for them. Even though others said things would not work out, they knew that God would make a way. After they prayed, they returned to the lobby where Tim and the Human Resources Director were waiting for them.

"We're not sure, but we think we can find a way to get a renewed visa if we can just speak with the corporate attorney," Chris stated.

Tim bit his lip as he seemed to be having a debate with himself over what he should do next.

"I'm afraid that's not my decision to make," he said after several moments, "You'll have to speak with the corporate office. They may not grant you permission, but at least you can ask."

They did as Tim had suggested, and by God's hand, they were allowed to speak with the attorney. He agreed to try looking into some alternate means of legally attaining a new visa. After submitting all the required documents to him, Grace and Chris waited anxiously to see if he could help them. They flew back to Michigan and though they had no results from the attorney yet, they were believing for God's favor and trusted Him to work things out. They began to act on their faith and started packing up their belongings.

The days turned to weeks and they still had not heard from the attorney, but God told them to plan a moving date regardless. Nervous, they did as He had said. In June, they were standing in church during worship, when the pastors declared that they were going to pray over Grace and Chris. The pastors did not know anything that had been going on, but as they laid hands on the couple, prophetic words began to come forth.

"Truly Son, you have been obedient to My call, that's why you see great grace upon your life. Know that this time as I send you to this new place, you are well equipped for what you are called to. It's not only the position in the natural you are set to do, I am also knitting some hearts whom I have positioned in that region for you to connect with as you have a work to do in that region and there will be a spiritual battle for you to fight. But fear not, I will link you up with those who have hearts to see the transformation in that region, to raise up the standard of worship so the heavens over that region will be split open for My glory to come to dwell. So be encouraged, as you set your heart to go, I want you to expect great joy to come.

For Son, you are one who is strong; there is great strength inside of you. I'll use you in ways that you could never imagine. Sometimes you think your wife hears from Me, but you don't; which is not true. Don't quench the Spirit I've placed inside of you, because you do hear from Me, and you're getting your daily marching orders.

Daughter, truly I feel your sorrow, and I feel your pain as you move from place to place. I know you wonder when you will be able to put the tent pegs in and settle down. But Daughter, truly your place is with Me, I am the living God who will carry you wherever you go. All you need to do is to follow. You will be that tent for your family, you will be that place for your husband to come for refuge, you will be the well to give out the water for him to drink from. And I am the source, darling. It will be never ending, always clear; it'll always be definite and clear. It will always be there for you. So fear not when you move from place to place and the civilization doesn't care for you, I care for you! Be strong and be in Me! Saith the Lord!

For you have wondered why I keep stretching you and why I keep putting you in uncomfortable places. I will say to you, I do so it's not because you did anything wrong, but because I desire to stretch you, and to mold you, to make you more pliable. For you were eager to set up your tent at different camps and stay put. Daughter, I'd have you to move forward with Me because there's much I desire to put in you.

You need not be afraid, because I am a good Shepherd, and the places I lead you to will be green pastures. I will be your all in all in those places. More importantly I will use those places to process you, and to make the changes I need to make inside of you, because there is a work I have for you to do. You will need to be adaptable to each every situation and I will also use you to minister in each and every situation.

In the place you are going, there are many people with wounded hearts. Daughter, you have the softness I placed within you that will be able to touch many cultures. Truly this is the place known as "Sin City," but daughter it'll be the place known by your hand as the "Healing City." For truly I have placed healing within your lips and healing in your hands. When you lay hands on people, you will see the healing anointing flowing from your hands to their physical body.

So be encouraged, Daughter! The places I lead you to, I am going there in front of you, I am going there beside you, and I am going there behind you. I will not abandon you. It's not that you have done any-thing wrong, it's because I desire to implement much in you. You and your husband will come to a place of unity to minister to many who come across your path. And the unity among your family members will increase as well, saith the Lord!"

All these years God had been training them to adapt to every situation and to trust Him when circumstances overwhelmed them. He would be with them as He brought them to the place He had prepared for them. That was all Grace needed to hear to regain full confidence that this was God's will and that, regardless of how the situations looked, He would come through for them as He always did. She felt very sorry for ever doubting Him.

Another month rolled by and it was now the first week of July. The expiration date on their visas was getting really close. Chris and Grace were still waiting for their attorney's update so when the phone rang, and Grace saw the caller ID showed it their Jewish attorney's name, her heart leaped!

"Hello, this is Grace, how are you Danny?" Grace said as she tried to calm herself down.

"Hey Grace, I am doing well. I have some news for you regarding the visas," Danny said in his usual cool lawyer tone that made it hard to tell whether it was good news or bad news.

"So what's the news?" Grace asked, finding it hard to breathe.

"Your efforts and persistence have paid off! Your new visas have been granted!" Danny said with an unusual excitement in his voice this time.

"Really? Oh my goodness! Praise God! You mean we have them, we can move to Las Vegas and Chris can take the job offer?" Grace shot off questions like a machine gun blast, "Oh, sorry Danny, I guess I asked too many questions all at once, but are we set?"

"Yes and yes to all your questions!" Danny chuckled, "Congratulations to you both. This case truly has been one of its kind! Your hard work in preparation really counted!"

Grace paused in her excitement and said, "No, Danny, it's not us, it is God who provides! It is His plan, not ours. This all proves prayer works! And of course we are thankful He sent an angel like you to help us out!"

"Hmmm, sure, well, I will be mailing you all the documents, have a smooth relocation to Nevada!" Danny was obviously hesitant to make any further comment.

Unbeknownst to Grace, after he hung up the phone, Danny sat in his high-rise office in Washington, D.C. and recalled the process he had gone through with Chris and Grace. "What kind of God are they believing in?" he thought to himself, "What a testimonial of their faith?! How on earth did they know the visas would come through for them?" These questions caused Danny to think deep thoughts about this unusual couple and their faith in God.

Grace and Chris celebrated that night and didn't waste any time booking the flights to their new location. They finished packing the boxes and rose early the morning of their flight to Las Vegas. Grace was excited that God had been so faithful to provide for them, but she was also nervous and a bit scared. After all, they were moving to Las Vegas, a city that thrived on blatant sin. Was this another step for them on their way through Egypt to their promised land?

Ask Yourself

- Have you "encountered" God in a very person way? If yes, how was it?

- How did you hold on to the words, the dreams, or the vision God revealed to you?

- What does this word "faith" mean to you exactly?

Chapter 16

Stepping into the Promised Land

W hile "Las Vegas" was known as a city of sin and the entertainment capitol of the world, Grace found out some things about Las Vegas quite different than what most people knew about it. According to the Official City of Las Vegas website:

"In about 1829, a young scout named Rafael Rivera was the first person of European ancestry to look upon the valley. His discovery of a valley with abundant wild grasses growing and a plentiful water supply reduces the journey by several days. The valley is named Las Vegas, Spanish for [The Meadows.]"

"Interesting...The Meadows!" Grace thought, "So, it was originally meant to be a place of abundant life and greenery!" In fact, Grace discovered that the world famous Las Vegas Strip was one of the smallest areas of the whole city of Las Vegas.

When they got to Las Vegas, they went to the hotel where Chris was working. After they took the weekend to settle in, the next course of action was to begin looking for a home. They arrived at a time when the real estate industry was at its peak. People were buying up homes within a week of when they were listed. They met with a realtor who took them to see some homes in the area.

After showing them the first house she asked, "Well? What do you think?"

"It's nice," Grace said, "but we'd like to keep looking."

Nancy, their realtor looked shocked by Grace's answer and then advised, "If you like the house, I wouldn't wait too long to make a decision. The homes on the market are in high demand right now, good property won't last long."

On their way to the next home, Grace noticed Nancy was wearing a cast on her leg. Grace felt God urging her to pray for Nancy, but she refused thinking it might embarrass her. After three days of house-hunting, they were looking at a lovely home in Henderson. Grace and Chris went to look around upstairs, while Nancy waited for them on the first floor. Grace was the first to come back downstairs and as she and Nancy waited for Chris, God again urged Grace to pray for Nancy's injury.

Reluctantly Grace asked, "I noticed you injured your leg. How did that happen?"

As Nancy began to relay her story and she shared how the doctors said she would have to have the cast on for several weeks, God once more spoke to Grace, "What are you waiting for?"

After Nancy had finished her story, Grace finally asked, "Are you a believer?"

"A believer of what?" Nancy asked somewhat cautiously.

"See, Lord? Now what do I say?" Grace silently asked.

"A believer in Christ," she clarified, praying she would have the right words to do what God was expecting of her.

"Yes, I am, big time!" Nancy responded proudly.

"So you don't mind if I pray over your leg?" Grace asked.

"Of course not, what took you so long to ask me?" Nancy replied with a smile.

A few days later, Nancy called Grace to tell her the doctors had just taken her cast off and they praised God together for this answer to prayer. Grace and Chris later purchased the house they had visited the day Grace prayed for Nancy.

The Gift of Healing

Over the next few months, the family visited over eleven churches and saw some very interesting things in each one. One church in particular stuck with Grace. It was on the top floor of a department store. The pastor wore a purple suit. Grace had seen black, white, beige, and gray suits before, but never purple! The suit was so vibrant that Grace had trouble focusing on anything else for the duration of the service. When the service had ended, Grace noticed one of the singers was in a wheelchair. She was sitting off in the corner alone. Grace again felt the unction to pray for healing. This time, she obeyed that small voice inside of her right away. She went over to the woman and introduced herself.

"Do you mind if I pray for you?" she then asked.

"Well, I've been prayed for many times by many different people, and it hasn't helped. But if you really want to, then I guess you can go ahead," the woman replied.

Reluctantly, Grace began to pray. Right away both women felt the Holy Spirit and when the prayer was done, Grace looked up to see the woman was shivering. Both began to cry and the woman thanked Grace as she shared she had never felt God's presence that strong before. In each of the eleven churches they visited, God had Grace pray for at least one person for healing. It did not take long for Grace to become comfortable with laying hands on people at random.

After visiting all but one of the churches on the list they had printed out of churches in Las Vegas, they had all but ruled out the last one because it was the furthest away from their home. However, after checking out every other option, Grace insisted that they go and see what it was like. They were desperate to find a church home, so that Sunday they visited the Church of the Living Word. They were pleasantly surprised to find that the worship was very charismatic and the teaching was powerful. It suited everything they had been looking for in a church. Even though it was so far away from their home, Grace knew this was their new church home for this season.

Months later, Grace signed up to attend the women's ministry group that met every Tuesday for eight weeks. Grace enjoyed it very much and decided she wanted to become more involved. Towards the end of the semester, Grace met with the women's ministry director, Carrie. Grace immediately felt the love and genuine care that Carrie had in her heart for all people. As they talked, Grace knew they would become close friends. Carrie sensed many great and powerful gifts inside of Grace. As she continued to witness Grace's servant's heart and passion for the Lord, she decided to make Grace a small group leader for the next semester. She did not know Grace had been a worship team and home fellowship leader at their former church.

As Chris and Grace started settling down in their new home in Henderson, Grace had the opportunity to build relationships with all the other executives' families. Each of the wives took turns hosting monthly gatherings for potluck meals or birthday parties. Grace didn't necessarily enjoy all the chit-chat about Hollywood celebrities, the newest clothes trends, or which movie star was sexier, she got to make some new friends and more importantly a chance to witness the love of God to these families without "preaching."

It didn't take long for some of these families to notice there was "something" special that contributed to Grace and Chris' strong marriage and their well-behaved children. One afternoon one of the women from the group, called Grace.

"Hey Grace, do you have a moment?" Katie asked.

"Yes, Katie. How are you?" Grace replied thinking this call was about the next gathering.

"I need someone to talk to," Katie said as she started crying.

"Are you okay? Where are you? Are you home?" Grace was concerned.

"I am home, but can Stephanie and I come over?" Katie asked, sounding desperate.

"Sure and do bring your little one over. Peter and Emily can keep her company while we talk," Grace offered lifting up a prayer for God's help as she spoke to her new friend.

Half hour later, Katie arrived with her toddler. Grace helped her settle her child down to play with Peter and Emily, then invited Katie to sit away from them and talk.

"Grace, how do you make your husband trust you?" Katie asked.

"What do you mean by that?" Grace asked, not at all sure what this was all about.

"Well, I never know how much money Jeff has, and if I asked him to buy something for the household, he always gives me this almost angry look. It's like he doesn't trust me to know about our finances," Katie described.

"So are you saying you guys don't have a shared bank account? You don't manage your finances together?" Grace asked as she tried to understand such an arrangement.

"No, he has his own account, and I have mine. When we got married, he told me he didn't want to have a shared account to keep things simple," Katie explained.

"And you agree to that?" Grace asked surprised that other couples did things so differently.

"Well, I thought he might change his mind afterwards," Katie said with tears in her eyes.

"So, obviously it has been this way for years," Grace said knowing they had been married for several years, "so what's your concern now?"

"Grace, after all these years, I just found out he's been receiving an annual bonus from the hotel!" Katie exclaimed.

Grace was shocked! It was always a time for their family to celebrate when Chris announced the bonus had been issued! It was normally a larger amount than the monthly salary!

"How did you find out this year?" Grace asked, trying to remain calm.

"I asked him for money to purchase some items for Stephanie's coming birthday party, but he said the money was tight right now. Then when I went to the hotel charity function with you and the other wives, I overheard how you and Chris were rejoicing about the wonderful bonus. I felt like such a fool!" Katie shared, obviously hurt and angered by her husband's deceit.

"Katie, I am so sorry to hear that," Grace said sincerely, "Have you tried to communicate with Jeff about this?"

"I did, but when I asked him about the bonus, he said that is was none of my business! And the next thing I know, I saw this on his desk in our home office," Katie sobbed as she handed a piece of paper to Grace.

"It looked like he purchased a..." Grace couldn't quite believe what she read from the paper.

"A diamond ring!" Katie shouted.

"Who would he buy a ring for?" Katie asked desperately, "Grace, I am afraid and angry at the same time! What should I do?"

"Katie, as bad as it looks, let's not make any quick assumptions. You guys really need to sit down and have an open honest conversation about everything! Then we can go from there," Grace said as calmly as she could.

"Grace, I called you because I've noticed that you seem to have very strong faith in God, do you mind praying for me and my family?" Katie asked hopefully.

"Absolutely, God knows exactly what you need, Katie. As you are willing to trust in Him, He will help you to see things with clarity and not make any hasty decisions," Grace assured her friend, privileged Katie trusted her enough to come to her in a time like this.

Grace prayed over Katie and her family, then for her marriage and for open communication between Katie and her husband. Weeks later, Katie shared the great news of what God had done as a result of this time of prayer.

"We are relocating to Florida," Katie told Grace, "Jeff got transferred there as promotion!"

"Congratulations, Katie!" Grace said, "I am so happy for you!"

"I wanted to thank you again for your prayer," Katie said warmly, "Jeff and I did have that open communication."

"How did it go?" Grace asked eagerly.

"He admitted he had an affair and had totally gotten off track with his life and his priorities. I kept my composure as you had encouraged me to and just listened to what he had to say," Katie shared, obvious proud of herself.

"And then what happened?" Grace asked knowing God must have done something amazing in this marriage.

"He said he was sorry and had already realized that it was a terrible mistake!" Katie explained, "Especially after he figured out the other women's true face! She wasn't really interested in him, she only wanted his money."

"So, then what did you do?" Grace asked anxious to hear the rest of the story.

"So we had that long over-due open conversation. He didn't realize the way he operated our finances bothered me that much. I hadn't really been up front with him about my feelings. I also found out more about myself in the process. Subconsciously my self-esteem was so low I really needed to know I was valuable enough to him that he would respect me and share every part of his life with me," Katie explained.

"Wow! Katie, that's some discovery!" Grace agreed, overwhelmed by how God had used her simple prayer to open up such wonderful communication between this couple.

"It is all because of you, Grace!" Katie declared as she held Grace's hands. "Your prayer, your encouragement, and more importantly the way you live your faith in front of me and our circle of friends has been very instrumental in saving my marriage!"

Grace really hadn't seen this was coming as she had obediently prayed with Katie that day, "I just share what I have experienced from God's love, it is God who does the work."

"I don't know your God much yet, but I am going to! You are such a living testimonial!" Katie said sincerely. "Don't let the other women in the circle stop you from living your faith walk in front of them. Though they may laugh at you, who knows, one day they might come to you to ask for prayer, just like I did."

Grace was so grateful to be able to touch another life this way! And Katie was right with her prediction about the other women in her circle. Over the next few years they came to Grace, one-by-one for direction and wisdom. Their gathering time became a lot more pleasant for Grace as the "gossip" stopped and these women started caring for one another and giving more to the causes they shared.

While Grace was giving back to whom ever God brought into her life, she was still waiting for her own mom's life to turn around. It was so encouraging seeing other people's lives being transformed through her prayer, but at the same time it had been frustrating watching her own mother continue living in such darkness. Grace knew she needed to do what God called her to do and when it came to her mom, she just needed to let go and let God!

The Gift of Teaching

At the church, Grace was glad that the women ministry gave her constant stimulation throughout the week as she fellowshipped with other women, and learned that she was not alone with the struggles that she faced. As the new semester began, she was in for a surprise as she was asked to lead a group by herself this time. Grace's initial excitement turned to anxiety. Though she loved mentoring the women, she questioned whether or not she would be able to do it on her own.

In the first group meeting, Grace spoke on prayer. She knew she had to be organized and tried to exude an air of confidence as she taught. She asked the women how often they prayed during the week, but each woman had a different excuse as to why they could not spend much time in prayer. This shocked Grace that very few ladies seemed to understand the value of prayer and how quick they were to disregard it. As Grace was driving home, God told her to share with the women her relationship with Him and what she had done even in the midst of her fourteen-hour working-day.

The next week, Grace said to the women, "You all say you can't pray because there's nowhere you can be alone, or because you are just too busy with other things. Well there's something you can do that I find very effective. Pray when you go to the bathroom."

All the women began to laugh.

"You laugh, but it works. Think about it. You always make time to go to the bathroom when you need to and it's perhaps the one place where you can truly be alone and undisturbed." Grace smiled as she added, "You're away from noise and you can really focus on God."

"Are you kidding?" asked one of the women in between chuckles.

"Do I look like I'm kidding?" asked Grace with a smile. "It may sound funny but it works! When I had to work fourteen hours a day at The Club, from five o'clock in the morning until seven in the evening,

I was constantly meeting with people. The only place and time I wasn't disturbed was when I was in the restroom. I often had some serious conversation with God during that time. Prayer is important and we all need to make it a prominent part of our lives. Just try it and see what happens."

The women agreed to do so and the next week when the women met again, Grace heard testimony after testimony of multiple breakthroughs the women had experienced that week because they prayed whenever they went to the bathroom. They were very loud and energetic. Though Grace didn't know it at the time, their laughter and enthusiasm carried over into the next room where Pastor Nicki and Carrie were.

"Whose group is that?" asked Nicki.

"Grace's," Carrie told her.

"Oh, is that the new girl?" Nicki asked curiously

"Well, she's not really new anymore," Carrie laughed.

"What are they doing over there?" Nicki asked.

"Being really happy," Carrie said with a smile.

Later in the semester, Grace went about her usual routine of randomly calling on someone to read the prayer requests aloud. She called on a woman named Charlotte who quickly refused. After the group ended and everyone was leaving, Charlotte approached Grace.

"Don't you ever do that to me again," she said angrily. "I don't like speaking in public and that was very embarrassing for me."

"Oh, I'm sorry I did not mean to embarrass you and I shall respect that from now on. But I feel God is telling you He wants you to break out of that place of fear," Grace replied graciously, though the woman just angrily stormed off.

The following week as they were about to close in prayer, Grace gathered up all of the prayer requests. There were three requests for healing from cancer. Grace had everyone close their eyes, but before she prayed God stopped her. She walked around the room until she reached Charlotte. Sensing that someone was standing beside her, Charlotte looked up. Her eyes widened as she saw Grace looking at her. She glared at Grace trying to warn her not to make her pray.

Grace bent down and whispered to her, "It is my job to tell you that your job is to pray for these cancer patients. You can accept it or decline. It is very easy for me to pray for these people myself, but it is not God's will today."

At this, Charlotte began to cry, "I told you I can't!"

All the other women gently encouraged her to pray. After several minutes, Charlotte agreed to give it a try. Her prayer began very softly, but the longer she prayed, the louder she grew. The Spirit of God immediately filled the room as Charlotte's prayers grew more powerful by the second. All the women began jumping up and down and praising God. Some were even crying.

"I did it!" Charlotte said with disbelief.

"Yes, you did and your prayer was so powerful!" said one of the group members, quickly joined by the rest of the group.

Charlotte came across the room and gave Grace a big hug, she whispered in her ear, "Thank You!"

Grace went through the rest of that day thanking God for His goodness as the whole group witnessed Charlotte's breakthrough. Even more amazing was the next time they met, there were three praise reports of cancers being healed that week! As word spread out, more and more people came to Grace asking for prayer for healing and mentoring.

Fulfillment of Prophecy – Part One

It was in the spring of 2007 when Grace got a surprising call from her mother in Taiwan.

Anne sounded different as she said excitedly, "Grace, I have something to tell you."

Not sure what to expect, Grace answered, "I'm listening, mom."

"Well," Anne continued with a definite lift in her voice, "I am to be baptized next Sunday."

Grace was not at all sure she heard what her mother had said correctly so she asked, "What did you say, mom?"

"I said, I will be baptized next Sunday here at my home church," Anne repeated, "I thought you'd be happy to know about it."

Grace was speechless as she tried to comprehend what she just had heard. Her initial shock turned to joy as she felt an overwhelming wave of gratitude for God's faithfulness!

"Grace, are you still there?" Anne asked, puzzled by the lack of response from her daughter.

"Yes, I am here! Mom, that is awesome!" Grace said once she regained control of her voice. "How did it happen? I mean how did you end up going to church, and making a decision to commit to God?"

"It started a few months ago," Anne slowly explained, "I passed a church, which I had visited once or twice when I was a young girl and I just felt drawn to it."

"Did you just say you visited a church before? I didn't know that?!" Grace asked, even more surprised by her mother's words.

"Yes, I did," Ann continued, "As I walked up the stairs, the closer I came to the Sanctuary, the more the tears started to flow down my face. I couldn't control it. I felt like a blanket of love was being wrapped around me. Finally, I made it to the altar and fell down on my knees!"

"Then what happened?" Grace asked encouraging her mother to continue.

"The pastor came and stood there quietly with me for a while. Then he just simply asked me, 'Are you ready to come home?'" Anne recounted with awe in her voice.

Grace's face was covered with tears of joy!

"I prayed the salvation prayer with the pastor, and he helped me to find a church closer to where I live now. I have been attending church since then. God also helped me to find a good paying babysitting job, too!" Anne announced happily.

"Hold on a minute," Grace interrupted, astonished that so much had happened in her mother's life since they had last spoken, "you found a church and you also got a job?! Why you didn't tell me any of this before? I am so happy for you, mom!"

"I always thought the God you talked about all these years was a foreigner," Anne tried to explain, "Maybe it was because you married a foreigner. Anyway, I thought you believed in a western culture God."

Grace thought, "I think we have a lot to catch up on," but she continued listening as her mother shared her journey to God.

"As I hit rock bottom, I was so low I had nowhere to turn but to God," Anne confessed, "then suddenly my eyes were opened and I was able to see what was really going on in my life."

"Mom," Grace said when her mother finished her amazing story, "I really don't know what to say, but that I am extremely happy for you! I thank God for His faithfulness, that after over ten years of praying for you, today I see one of my dreams came to pass in such a miraculous way! I am in awe of what God has done for all of us!"

Grace knew it was part of the "Promised Land" God had told her about in the Michigan prophecy that had now come to pass! While she had been obedient in a foreign land, God had taken care of her mom!

Providence

After serving the church for another four years, both Grace and Chris sensed God was calling them to establish something else. Grace and Chris were very involved with the couples' ministry and held a small group at their home. It had been three years since they first moved into that house and they knew they needed more space. They asked God for a new home that would be within their $420,000 dollar budget.

Chris's hotel had a position open up when Tim was transferred. Since God had told Chris and Grace that promotion was coming soon, they just naturally expected that the, "Not one step but three" promotion was at hand. They both felt that when it happened the Hotel would sponsor Chris to apply for his Green Card (at the hefty expense of $12,000), finally ending the nightmare of working visas, and then they could look for a larger home.

One morning as Grace was journaling and praying, she flipped to a page in her journal from 2006. God dropped the word, "providence" in her heart. She jotted it down and went to a dictionary and found it meant, "God's divine care; Economical management, Cost little." She had no clue as to what God was trying to tell her, so she filed it away knowing God would reveal His purpose soon enough.

One Sunday not long after this word was given to Grace, the family stopped by a gas station to get gas and Chris bought a copy of the Sunday newspaper. That afternoon as they enjoyed their usual Sunday afternoon coffee and sat reading the paper, Grace flipped to the Real Estate page. There at the top of a gigantic full-page ad, "PROVIDENCE" jumped off the page at her!

"My goodness!" Grace exclaimed as she showed the paper to Chris.

"So this is your 'providence'?" Chris said with a smile.

"We'd better check it out," Grace said knowing if it was from God they would know soon enough.

It turned out "Providence" was a large master-planned community on the other side of the town from where they lived that was being built by seventeen different builders. For two years, Grace and Chris drove to Providence to see whether there was a "dream home" for them, but they didn't find anything to suit their needs and remain in their budget. It was in May of 2008 when one Monday morning, both Chris and Grace felt led to drive to Providence to the area of one particular builder. The advertisement in the newspaper seemed to fit with what they are looking for. While they were on the main road of the community on the way to that builder, suddenly they saw a large sign from another well-known builder indicating his homes also fit their needs.

"Honey, since we have driven this far, why not go in and take a look?" Grace suggested.

After they conversed with the sales representative, they found there was only one empty lot and the model home left in this sub-community. They found themselves at "home" in the model home. The layout, the size, the quality, the interior design, the kitchen—everything seemed to be exactly what they had been looking for. The builders had "by chance" decorated the two smaller bedrooms as a girls' room and a boy's room. The one was custom painted with white and pink stripes with flower border, and the other a bold blue and red with motorbikes wall paper. They were perfect for Emily and Peter! Everything they could have asked or dreamed of was in this one house.

When Grace walked out to the backyard, she found she could overlook the Las Vegas strip to the right and view the beautiful desert mountains to the left. She was in awe of the spectacular view from this backyard. As she started praying in her heart to ask God about the house, a butterfly flew by and gently rested on her shoulder.

"Change is coming, Grace! Just like a caterpillar transforms into a butterfly, it is total transformation; be ready for the transformation!" Grace sensed God was talking to her intimately.

As she walked back into the house, she saw Chris was sold on the five-burner stove top.

"So, what do you think Honey?" Grace smiled at Chris.

"I think it's the one," Chris replied, "if God solves two little problems."

"You mean the asking price and our current home?" Grace asked, already knowing what they had discussed.

"Yes," Chris replied, "We both know it's not a good time to sell because of the current economic situation."

"Then God will have to provide very good tenants for our house and a down payment at our desired price," Grace confirmed.

After two hours in this house, they left with a confidence in their heart that this was the home they were to have. Though they had no idea how God could slash the price from $499,000 to $420,000, find a good tenant for their current house, and supply the 20% down payment on this house without having to borrow from the bank—all in less sixty days.

As they went home to seek confirmation, Grace asked Emily, "If you could choose to re-decorate your room, how would you do it?"

"Mom, I'd love to have white and pink stripes like the beautiful scrapbooking paper you have, and maybe with a flower border all around," Emily said clearly painting her a mental picture.

Grace and Chris looked at each other with smile. They knew it was the house God had prepared for them. So they started taking action to do what they could do, and the rest...they left to the Lord.

Grace took some nice photos of their current home and posted them with a free classified listing. She didn't even place a sign in their front yard as they didn't want to deal with bunch of strangers knocking on the door. In less than three weeks, they received an overwhelming response to their ad and successfully rented their home to a wonderful military family. On the other hand, Chris's promised promotion seemed farther and farther away. With their visa renewal date quickly approaching, it seemed to them that God would have them spend their own money and do a self-sponsored Green Card application.

By faith, they followed what they sensed from God and hired the same attorney who helped them relocated from Michigan to Las Vegas to start the application process. Grace and Chris were told it would take at least two years to know the result, but they would be able to stay in the country until the result was finalized, even after their current visas expired. With tenants secured, Grace and Chris sought some professional knowledge from their Realtor friends about how to bargain down the price and terms with the builder. In less than four weeks, they were able to negotiate the asking price down to $420,000 as the builder was eager to sell out the very last house in the community. Chris and Grace knew they were right on the track with God.

They didn't want to borrow the down payment from the bank, so Chris called his father to explain the situation to him. Without the same level of faith in the family, Chris had no idea how it would turn out.

"Would you be interested in investing in some property out here, Dad?" Chris asked.

"With the current US economy, absolutely not! The market is too unstable to invest in right now," his father responded, "but I'll tell you what, since I helped your sister with the down payment on her home and I want to be fair, I'll do the same for you and you can pay me back later."

Overjoyed, Chris lavished his father with thanks, and then went to tell Grace. The couple wasted no time in making preparations to meet with the sales representative and do the paper work to purchase their new house. God had indeed done an awesome work on all sides for them!

"Now we have the house, our Green Cards are in process, Lord, where is Chris' promotion?" Grace was wondering in her heart.

Two weeks before Christmas, as they were packing up and getting ready for their trip to Switzerland for a long-planned Christmas vacation, Chris came home earlier than usual.

"Hey Honey, are you okay?" Grace asked surprised at his unplanned early arrival.

"Papa, Papa, you are home early!" his children screamed as they joyfully ran and hugged him.

"Hey guys, give me a couple of moments with mom, okay?" he said hugging each of them before sending them off to their rooms.

"Ok, but will you play with us later on?" Peter asked.

"Of course!" Chris said but his smile looked forced to Grace.

After the children went upstairs to their rooms, Chris and Grace sat down at the dinning table.

"So, what's going on?" Grace asked, though she didn't like what she was sensing.

"They let me go," Chris finally said sadly. "They explained it was a business decision because the hotel is not doing good financially."

"But you are the one holding everything in operations together!" Grace responded, "Aren't they seeing that?"

"Well, I don't think that mattered much," Chris reflected, "even after eight years of working hard for them, too."

"Oh, honey, I am sure God has a better plan for you and for our family!" Grace said as she tried to encourage Chris and herself at the same time.

She was really trying to understand what God was doing. Hadn't He said we'd be in our Promised Land and with amazing promotions? Hadn't they done everything obediently?

"I guess all we can really do is go enjoy our vacation, and then see what God is up to," Chris suggested, also wondering what God had in mind.

"Sounds like a plan," Grace agreed managing to smile as they finished their packing and went ahead with their plans to visit their family in Switzerland.

Ask Yourself

- Have you been promised a move into the Promised Land?

- Have your ideas of how this would happen been aligned with God's? Grace's ideas were in a reversed order. She thought promotion would lead to Green Card sponsorship, then they would have more money to buy the larger home.

- What do you think about the decision of Grace's taking on Charlotte's weakness?

Chapter 17

Officially Granted! Time to Take the Land

I n Switzerland, Grace and Chris eagerly continued to ask God whether they should move back to Switzerland or if He had something else in mind. Knowing that the prophecy hadn't been fully manifested yet, they diligently sought to know His plan.

During their devotional time, there was a portion of scripture in **Genesis 26** that kept coming up.

"Now there was a famine in the land—besides the previous famine in Abraham's time—and Isaac went to Abimelek king of the Philistines in Gerar. The LORD appeared to Isaac and said, "Do not go down to Egypt; live in the land where I tell you to live. Stay in this land for a while, and I will be with you and will bless you. For to you and your descendants I will give all these lands and will confirm the oath I swore to your father Abraham."(Genesis 26:1-3)

"It sounds like we need to stay put in Vegas," Chris suggested.

They read on as Isaac obeyed God, pitched his tent and dug wells.

"From there he went up to Beersheba. That night the LORD appeared to him and said, [I am the God of your father Abraham. Do not be afraid, for I am with you; I will bless you and will increase the number of your descendants for the sake of my servant Abraham.] Isaac built an

altar there and called on the name of the LORD. There he pitched his tent, and there his servants dug a well." (Genesis 26:23-25)

"That day Isaac's servants came and told him about the well they had dug. They said, "We've found water!" He called it Shibah, and to this day the name of the town has been Beersheba." (Genesis 26:32-33)

"Multiple wells, multiple streams of income to help people in need!" Grace said.

Suddenly she felt like everything clicked. For years she'd had no idea why God had led her to continue studying MBA, internet marketing, and network marketing courses. She had even started to create some streams of income here and there putting into practice the things she was learning. As the economy went down, Grace knew her knowledge would be able to help many people start up their own businesses even as there was a "famine in the land"!

When they returned from vacation, Chris and Grace started reorganizing their goals, business and schedule. For Chris, it was quite refreshing to be able to attend his kids' field trips after all these years of living on a corporate career oriented schedule. They also started their family devotion time. What amazed Chris and Grace was they were not the only ones maturing in spiritual growth. Both Emily and Peter were often given dreams and visions, and the accuracy often left their parents speechless. The biggest concern for them was the Green Card application, but all they could really do was wait patiently and cast the burden on God. As they waited, suddenly they realized why God asked them to self-sponsored to apply Green Cards! Otherwise, as Chris was let go from his job, the family would have to leave the country in 2 weeks!

The Marketing Hat

Grace started picking up her "marketing hat" again. She began to build up various businesses with her old friend and mentor Amy, as she started to realize that her calling of healing was to reach beyond the church walls and into the market place. She was especially called to empower women who had wounds and emotional baggage to move forward in their lives via building their own businesses. Instead of bringing them to church, she brought "church" to them as she walked the walk! More and more entrepreneurs from different walks of life, nationalities, and beliefs were attracted to Grace as she gave from her heart, and allowed them to shine!

Just like everyone else, Chris and Grace faced the challenge of a tight budget and shrinking cash flow. It was tough to stay walking in faith when they weren't even sure they would be able to stay in the country. There were times of weakness when they would go to God on their knees seeking reassurance and encouragement from their heavenly Father.

"Lord, how will we be able to make it? Are we on the right track?" Grace asked God.

One day Peter popped a question that Grace had no idea had been plaguing her young son, "You and Papa will stay together, right?"

"Of course, we will," Grace quickly answered, stunned by his question. "Why would you ask such a kind of question?"

"I am afraid because there are some parents of my friends who got divorced after their dad lost his job," Peter confided in his mom.

"Peter, I assure you we will stay together and love each other no matter what," Grace said as she hugged Peter tightly.

It was spring time when their old friend Amy came from Singapore to visit. It was a happy reunion after so many years.

"So, what do you guys need in this household that you didn't buy yet?" Amy asked them after their Sunday morning breakfast.

"What do you mean?" Grace asked, puzzled by Amy's question.

"On the flight from Singapore, the Lord told me there was a large household item you guys meant to purchase, but due to budget cutbacks you have put it on hold. I am the one given the privilege to bless you with the item," Amy said with a big smile on her face.

Chris and Grace looked at each other and couldn't believe what they just heard. With trembling heart, Grace went to office to grab a piece of paper and gave it to Amy.

"It is a TV?" Amy asked as she looked at the paper and laughed.

"We were planning to purchase this specific TV after we did a lot of research. Since money is tight, it is not a priority at all, so we put it aside," Grace explained.

"I know how you guys sow money to the poor and needy, even if it means you have no money to buy your own stuff. When was the last time you guys shopped for clothes for yourselves?" Amy demanded.

"It was looooooong time ago!" Peter said with loud voice.

"All right, today it's Christmas time for this family," Amy proclaimed. "We are going to shop for everything you need. We need to dress you guys up and get ready for business!"

"Amy, you really don't have to do this," Chris said trying to persuade Amy that they were fine.

"Hey, be careful what you are trying to do, Chris! Don't rob my joy and blessing away!" Amy said not giving Chris a chance for any second thoughts. "You need to learn to be a receiver today."

So off they went as Amy blessed the family with sets of clothes, toys, and of course that 42-inch flat screen TV! Having been "givers" for decades, it was hard for Grace and Chris to be on the receiving end for a change. Words couldn't describe their gratitude for God's love and attention to even the smallest details of their lives. It served as a reminder that they were on the right track and God was with them all the time!

Time flew and it really was Christmas time. The family was still believing in faith for their Green Cards when one morning, seven-year-old Peter made a bold declaration.

"The green cards are in the mail, mom!"

Grace was in a dilemma. She was concerned if the Green Cards were not in the mail today, then it might hurt Peter's faith. At the same time, she wanted to believe today was indeed the day!

"Peter, that's awesome!" Grace told her son, trying to be diplomatic. "I know our Green Cards are coming, I am just not sure which day it will be."

"No, mom! God told me it's today!" Peter insisted. "Go check the mailbox, they will be there!"

Grace didn't know what else to say or do except walked to the mailbox and pray very hard! She opened the mailbox and as she sorted it through, there were three envelops from the Homeland Security Department. Graces' hands were shaking! After nearly two years of waiting, she felt like she was holding their future in her hands! She waited until Chris got home and handed him the envelopes.

"So this is it!" Chris said as he stared at the envelopes.

"I think so," Grace said as Peter and Emily nervously waited for their father to open the envelopes.

As Chris opened the first envelop, he quickly read it through. A smile started to appear on his face as he handed the letter to Grace. She carefully read it through line-by-line. When she saw the word, "Congratulations" she was in tears! Their permanent residency, their Green Cards had been approved! It was indeed the best Christmas gift they had ever received!

"I told you!" Peter said with a big smile.

With their Green Cards in hand, Grace knew Chris' "promotion" was at hand, however it would be up to God, when and how He would orchestrate it. More importantly she would see Las Vegas become the City of Healing in her lifetime! That evening, after the kids went to bed, Grace stepped out into their backyard where she could overlook the Las Vegas Strip and the beautiful dessert mountains.

Looking up towards the starry sky she spoke to God, "Who am I, Lord, that You, the God who created the whole Universe, including the Earth where I am living, are mindful of me? A little dot compared to the whole spectrum of the universe, I am much less than some tiny particle of dust, yet You come and adopt me as Your daughter, and find every opportunity to spoil me with Your blessings!"

Grace was filled with gratitude as she expressed her heart to God. Suddenly, she felt someone tapping her on the shoulder. She turned around, but there was nobody there. As she looked up to the sky again, "someone" tapped her again and she started hearing an audible voice:

"Grace, that's why I have been with you each single step of the way. In fact I have always been ahead of you, and behind you as well. I know one day your life will be the perfect example of My grace because I have embedded grace inside of you: Grace of Encouragement, Grace of Love, Grace of Wisdom, Grace of Healing, Grace of Worship, Grace of Leadership, Grace of Life! Now it's time for you to go out there to spread the message of My grace! For I love you My daughter and I love My people dearly!"

Trembling all over her body, Grace realized her Heavenly Father had just visited her in person! She dropped down on her knees with streams of tears flowing down her cheeks and thanked her Father God. She knew she was in her Promised Land!

This is not the end; this story is to continue about, "A Little Girl Called Grace!"

Ask Yourself

- Do you believe in the principle of "sowing and reaping"? Have you been a giving person? How does giving to others make you feel?

- Have you faced any financial challenge in life? If yes, have you found "receiving" is easy or difficult for you?

- Have you ever experienced or encountered God in the intimate way Grace did? What does that experience do for your faith walk?

Epilogue

G race's unwavering faith, reverence, and her intimate relationship with God allowed her to be a shining light for Christ wherever she went. Through hard work and obedience to God's calling
in her life, Grace has become a sought after speaker, leader, coach
and mentor for many in the market place. She has continually
brought the message of grace and hope to those she meets.

The core value of Grace's message is to empower women of all
generations by awakening their consciousness so they too can know
how valuable they really are; so valuable that the God of universe
was willing to die for them!

Grace's living testimonial has become the "Bible" for many to
read, as they witness Grace's life unfold! They have sensed God's
love for them intimately through Grace's willingness to walk the
walk of faith.

Grace's children have played a huge role in her life. They have
been one of her strongest lights. Grace continues to train them to
be sensitive to the Spirit of God, and in doing so, they continue to
bless her every day. They have been shining lights to other family
members whose belief in God is not yet as strong as theirs. Grace
continues to be aware of her children's walk with God. She helps

them to grow in Him so that they can know His voice when the day comes when Grace is no longer beside them.

Grace does not necessarily announce her own faith to others, for she wants others to be able to see Christ in her simply through her conduct. Only after they speak with her or witness her actions will they discover that she is a Christian. She firmly believes that we never know who is watching us, so she lives every moment for God.

Grace continues to walk in victory and joy. She walked out of the darkness from her past so that she could be brought into the light and become a light to those who are still in darkness. Her story encourages people, specifically women, to do those things that they may think are impossible. Her story exemplifies the truth that if God has placed a desire in your heart, He will help you to fulfill that desire no matter who tells you that you can't. Anything can be achieved through Christ, but everything we do should be done for Him. Grace's life does not end with this book. Her story continues...only by grace.

Will you let God lead you by His grace?

About the Author

K elly Baader, author of the widely popular, "A Little Girl Called Grace," is considered a pioneer in Entrepreneurial Coaching and Mentoring. She helps entrepreneurs to achieve wholeness in life; spiritually, physically, and financially through her transparent leadership style.

Just like many people, Kelly experienced ups and downs in life, especially as she grew up in a female discriminated environment. Though she went through a dysfunctional childhood, was nearly raped, and then walked in and out of a wrong marriage relationship—heavily wounded mentally, spiritually, and financially—she turned it around and became one of the top income earners in the hospitality industry by the time she was thirty. Since then she has impacted thousands of people's life, especially women, through her book, seminars and online courses!

Kelly is a sought after speaker, coach, and business consultant. Her true passion is to activate and ignite the passion inside of women, to empower and equip them to break free from all self-imposed limits and bondages, and allow the little girl inside of them to come out and play!

To learn more about Kelly, please visit http://KellyBaader.com or http://ALittleGirlCalledGrace.com and be sure to subscribe to her empowering newsletter to get her most updated posts and news.